Harmonic Horizons

Exploring the Art of Song Composition

by

Emeson E. Nwolie

Table of Contents

Introduction

So, you're itching to serenade the stars or churn out a chart-topper, are you? Welcome to the start of a thrilling escapade into the heart of melody and the soul of verse. Consider this a backstage pass to the secrets of crafting songs that could, quite possibly, resonate through time and space. We're not just stringing chords and scribbling lines here; we're stitching soundscapes with the threads of human experience. In this tome, you'll plunge into the mystique of songwriting, emerging not just with a toolkit for composition but with the spirit of creativity that calls melodies into being. Roll up your sleeves; it's time to weave your own aural tapestry, one that vibes with the rhythm of life and flows with the cadence of your own unique voice.

Chapter 1:
The Essence of Songwriting

Imagine songwriting as a hearty stew of emotion, rhythm, and narrative, simmering on a stove of sheer creativity—it's complex, flavourful, and nourishing to the soul. Within these melodic confines, we begin our journey to unpack the craft that has serenaded centuries and sparked revolutions of the heart. Songwriting isn't just about stringing chords and words together; it's a vibrant tapestry woven with threads of human experience, a language that speaks when plain words falter. In this chapter, we'll delve into the enigmatic core of song composition, exploring its dual nature as both an expressive art and a meticulous craft. Remember, songs are vessels cruising through the ocean of our thoughts, and every wave they ride, every breeze they catch, is a choice—a stroke of a painter's brush. And while we won't dissect the detailed anatomy of a melody line or the bones of rhythmic syncopation just yet, we'll begin by appreciating the elusive magic that makes a song not just heard, but felt. This is where we attune our senses to the ineffable rhythm of the universe and prepare to compose its whisperings into an opus that resonates with the pulse of life itself.

Defining Song Composition is akin to sketching a map of a land not yet discovered. It's an expedition into the heart of expression, where melodies tangle with harmonies, and words become the stepping stones for the listener's journey. It's more than just setting words to music; it's manifesting sentiments into sound, fashioning an audible tapestry that resonates with the human experience.

Imagine for a moment, you've stumbled upon a well of emotions, ideas flutter like leaves in an autumn breeze, waiting to be caught. Those are the seeds of your song. Composition is the careful cultivation of these seeds. It's about nurturing them with thoughtful musical choices; deciding when a whisper of a piano speaks louder than a crescendo of guitars; knowing when the silence between two notes holds the story's key.

At its core, a song is a delicate blend of three elements: melody, harmony, and rhythm. But these are mere skeletons until you breathe life into them with your individual spirit and creativity. The composition is your playground, the space where these elements dance to the rhythm you set, harmonize with the melody you create, and resonate with the lyrics you pen down.

When we talk about the composition, we're adventuring far beyond the simplicity of a catchy tune. We're diving deep into how a song feels. It's about movement and stillness, tension and release, the ebb and flow of musical storytelling. And while this may sound weighty, like a grand piano hanging by a thread, fear not. The beauty of composition lies not in complexity, but in the authentic expression of your artistic vision.

Casting magic into the mix, rhythm is the heartbeat of your song. It's the bones upon which everything is built. Whether it's a steady thump or an erratic pulse, rhythm is at the helm, steering the ship through turbulent and tranquil waters alike. It's the invisible force that makes you tap your foot, sway your body, feel the music in your bones.

Now, let's not forget melody, for it is the voice of your song. It's the golden thread running through the fabric of your composition, the charmer swaying listeners into a serenade of highs and lows. A potent melody can evoke tears or summon laughter, reminding us of forgotten moments, or propelling us into undiscovered futures.

But what is a body without its spirit? This is where harmony comes into play. Like a true companion to melody, it adds depth and color, bringing warmth to the coldness, and a melody to its fullest expression. Harmonies are the whispers in the background, the shades that turn a sketch into a masterpiece.

As you compose, bear in mind that every song tells a story. Your composition is the vessel for that story. It's not merely about stringing chords together or finding a rhyme for 'love'. It's about creating a narrative arc within your music, a journey that captivates and enthralls from the first note to the last.

Within the bounds of song composition, there exists a playground for experimentation. Rules are, at best, loose guidelines. A four-chord pop song can soar on the charts while an avant-garde piece confuses, yet moves, the audience in inexplicable ways. Innovation is born when you colour outside the lines, when you juxtapose the blues with electronic synths, all for the thrill of creating something fresh.

This journey of song composition is deeply personal yet strikingly universal. It's a vast sea where your individuality meets the collective consciousness of those who listen. Each song you pen is a ripple that can turn into a wave, influencing emotions, cultures, and even generations.

And remember, the tools of composition are but extensions of your vision. Instruments are messengers of your intent, be it the mournful violin or the jubilant ukulele. The texture and timbre of each instrument you select add to the palette from which you'll paint your auditory picture.

Yet, composition isn't a linear path. It's not a route walked in a straight line, but a meandering path where the best vistas may be found in unexpected detours. You may start with a lyric, a beat, or a melodic snippet—it's your path to forge, your tale to tell.

In the end, song composition is about connection. It's the bridge between your soul and that of your listener. When those notes ripple through the air and tap into the listener's heart, you've not only found a tune; you've found resonance. And in that moment, your composition transcends mere notes on a page and becomes part of someone's life soundtrack.

So take a breath, trust in your creativity, and let the symphony of ideas within you flow. For in the realm of composition, you are not just a songwriter; you are a weaver of dreams, a sculptor of silence, a maestro of the intangible. It's time to set your inner world to music and let it soar on the wings of composition.

As you embark on this intimate voyage of song composition, take solace in knowing that through the cacophony of life's orchestra, your song has the power to sing out, clear and true. It can make the heart soar, the spirit waltz, and gift the world with a melody that whispers tales of your unique universe. Embrace the challenge, relish the process, and the art of composition will become your trusted confidant on this wondrous journey of musical exploration.

Songwriting as an Art and Craft weaves its way into the heart of every songwriter, straddling the line between spontaneous inspiration and meticulous technique. It's a dance, quite literally, between the raw and the refined, the chaos and the order. There's a soulful rhythm to crafting a song that resonates; it's an intimate tango with words, melody, and harmony that, when done well, seems almost effortless.

Songwriting, you see, is an art form steeped in personal expression. It's about putting your soul on display, wearing your heart on your sleeve, and often reveals more about you than a diary ever could. There's a vulnerability in sharing your innermost thoughts and feelings through melodies and lyrics that connect with others on a profound level.

But let's not get it twisted; songwriting is also a craft. Like a potter at a wheel, it requires a deft touch, an understanding of form, and oftentimes, a tolerance for getting one's hands dirty. It's practicing chords until your fingers are nimble, honing your lyrical prowess until metaphors become second nature, and crafting melodies that stick like gum to the bottom of a school desk.

Imagine composition as an art. A blank canvas that tempts the brush, a silent piano before the first chord strikes. It's where originality and intuition rule the day, where the muse is not only welcomed but actively courted with the finest wines of the spirit. Every song begins as a spark of artistry, a moment of 'what if', an auditory daydream. It's the birthplace of hit singles and acoustic lullabies alike.

But as you wade deeper into the waters of songwriting, don't mythologize the process more than you should. While art is the vision, craftsmanship is the vehicle that brings your ideas into the world with clarity and finesse. It's knowing the rules well enough to bend them or, when the song calls for it, to break them with gusto.

Craftsmanship is all about the tools—and you've got quite a few at your disposal. Structuring a song isn't just a matter of pouring your heart out into a mic; it's mapping out a journey for the listener. It's setting a stage for your story with introductions, peaks, valleys, and, if you fancy, a grand finale that leaves them wanting more.

This delicate balance is especially evident in the relationship between melody and lyrics. The best songs seem to marry the two in a kind of perfect union that strikes listeners at their core. A great phrase paired with the right note can indeed be greater than the sum of its parts. It's a craft to find that sweet spot, and it takes equal measures of patience and experimentation.

Now, don't get lost in the notion that songwriting is purely a solitary endeavor, the reserve of lone wolf types howling at the muse. Collaboration is a craft in its own right. Working with others can sharpen your skills, introduce new perspectives, and challenge you to write outside your comfort zone. It's the art of open-hearted communication and shared vision.

Even as you venerate the art of songwriting, never underestimate the necessity of craft—the practice, the editing, the polishing until your song shines. It's in the rewrites that good songs often become great, in the honing of every line until they can stand proudly on their own, then seamlessly in the song's tapestry.

While songwriting can sometimes feel akin to catching lightning in a bottle, there's logic and learning in its pursuit. Studying the work of others isn't mere imitation, but a gateway to understanding the language of music at a deeper level. It's in the analysis of classic hits and the dissection of contemporary anthems that one can uncover the time-tested principles that frequently herald success.

And let's not forget the times when songs seem to write themselves, when every chord and melody falls into place with uncanny ease. Cherish these moments, but know they are the sweet fruits of all you've nurtured in the garden of your craft. For every effortless hit, there are countless hours of unseen labour, drafts tossed aside, and tunes hummed into the void, inviting the elusive spark of art to strike.

So, as you embark on this journey of melding art with craft, let your passion for songwriting be the flame that keeps you returning to the forge. Respect the craft as your toolbox, a repository of techniques and wisdom from those who've walked the path before you. And nurture the art as your north star, the unique voice that only you can bring to the world's vast choir.

In the art and craft of songwriting, you are the alchemist at the crossroads of heart and hand, creator and technician, weaving tapestries of sound that can move the soul. And in this dance between the ethereal and the tangible, you'll find not just songs, but pieces of yourself, ever unfolding, ever evolving, set to the timeless rhythm of human feeling.

To this end, embrace the songs yet to come, for each is a lesson, a story, a part of the tapestry you are yet to weave. They await your artistry, your craftsmanship, your voice. Let them be bold, let them be tender, but above all, let them be true.

So go ahead, let your fingers caress the keys, let your pen race across the page, and remember: in the art and craft of songwriting, every note, every word, every pause, has the potential to echo in someone's heart, including your own. It's the ultimate gift, the legacy of the songwriter — and it's in your hands.

Chapter 2:
Harnessing Your Musical Imagination

Segueing smoothly from the foundational concepts laid out in our exploration of songsmithery's essence, let's delve intrepidly into the nitty-gritty of sparking that inner fire – the musical imagination. Now, envisage a playground where the swings are melodies and the slides are harmonies; this is where we unleash the symphonies in our minds! It's about letting your thoughts pirouette to the rhythm of possibility, tapping into that latent concoction of memory, emotion, and sheer whimsical inspiration. Imagine a veritable cauldron where ideas simmer and bubble, waiting for you to stir in a dash of daring and a pinch of passion. Whether you're a shower-crooner-turned-composer or a maestro seeking fresh zest, let's finesse the craft of tending to the creative spark within. We're talking about priming the pump and letting the river of innovation flow, except here, your oar is a pen, and the rapids are your bursting, vibrant thoughts. So, let's dive into the thrilling odyssey of moulding the intangible into the unforgettable, shaping the echoes of your spirit into songs that resonate with the heartbeats of others.

Cultivating Creativity is akin to tending a garden within the soul where melodies can sprout from seeds of silence and lyrics can weave through the trellises of thought. As songwriters, the nurturing of this creative plot is paramount. So, let's roll up our sleeves and dig into the fertile soil of imagination, shall we?

First, it is essential to understand that creativity does not obey the ticking of the clock or the command of a schedule. Just like the heartbeats of a drum, it's got its own rhythm. Nevertheless, you can set the stage for it to flourish by creating a routine. A simple daily practice of picking up an instrument, doodling some chords, or penning down random lyrical ideas can act as a call to the muses that you're ready to play.

It's also crucial to create a workspace that invites creativity. Whether it's a corner of your bedroom with a guitar stand and a notebook, or a cozy nook with a keyboard and some fairy lights – make it your haven. It's like setting the table for an intimate dinner, except your guest is the creative force within you.

Don't be afraid to experiment, either. Blend genres, play with odd time signatures, or write a song from the perspective of a character. Step out of your comfort zone. It's like tossing a dash of Cajun spice into a stew – it might just be the kick that ignites a fresh, fiery idea.

Collaboration can be a highly effective way to water the seeds of creativity. Working with others combines various experiences and influences, creating a rich compost from which new ideas can grow. You could be just a jam session away from the next big hit.

Mistakes and imperfections should be embraced. Sometimes, hitting a wrong note can lead you down a path to a perfect melody. Think of it as a dance where stepping on each other's feet occasionally is part of the process—the dance of creation, unpredictable and beautiful.

And please, don't let the blank page intimidate you. It's not an abyss gazing into your soul. Jot down whatever crosses your mind, even if it seems nonsensical. Lyrics can often emerge from the soup of seemingly irrelevant ideas, much like a phoenix rising from a pile of disparate ashes.

To stay inspired, keep feeding your senses. Read voraciously, listen intently, and observe keenly. Art in all its forms is interconnected, with the power to elicit emotions and thoughts that can translate into music. It's like cross-pollination in nature, where different flowers give rise to new and beautiful hybrids.

Take breaks when you need to. Imagine your creativity as a well – it needs to be replenished. Sometimes the best way to fill it back up is to walk away and come back when the water's clear. When your mind is rested, new ideas can flow freely, without the muddy disturbance of fatigue.

Embrace the art of doing nothing as well. Ideas often come at the most unexpected times, like while you're sipping tea and staring at the rain. Creativity can strike when your guard is down and your mind drifts. It's in these quiet moments that the whispers of new tunes can be heard.

Don't compare your creative journey to others. Your voice, your stories, and your songs are uniquely yours. Comparison can be the thief of joy and the strangler of originality. Focus on cultivating your creative garden, and let others tend to theirs. The world needs the flavours you bring to the music feast.

Travel, if you can, literally or through the pages of books, the frames of movies, or the strokes of paintings. New experiences are like sunlight and rain for your creative garden. They make it lush, colourful, and full of life.

Be patient with yourself. Some ideas need time to germinate before they sprout into full songs. You can't rush a seed to grow faster; similarly, you can't force an idea before its time. Trust in your own process.

Record everything. Every hum, chord progression, or lyrical snippet could be the beginning of something beautiful. Reviewing these fragments later might unearth a gem that was laying in wait. Consider it like capturing butterflies—they may not seem significant on their own, but together, they create a kaleidoscope of potential.

Lastly, believe in the magic of your creativity. Confidence can cultivate the most barren of fields. Have faith in your abilities and let that confidence be the sun that shines down on the buds of your musical aspirations. Witness as they bloom into tempestuous symphonies and delicate ballads that are born from deep within you.

Let's remember, the aim here isn't to reinvent the wheel but to oil and decorate it to spin in a way that it plays your unique tune. Cultivating creativity is an ongoing, joyful challenge—one that requires tender care, patience, and above all, the belief that within you lies an orchard of musical possibility, just waiting to bear fruit. So grab that spade, fellow song crafter, and let's grow some symphonies.

Inspiration and Where to Find It

Now, let's get down to brass tacks. We've waxed lyrical about the art and craft of songwriting, but where does the spark that lights the bonfire of creativity come from? That, my friends, is the golden question that has sent many a musician on a wisdom-filled quest. You see, inspiration is a slippery customer—it doesn't keep office hours, and no two people find it in the same spot twice.

Sometimes, inspiration might hit you like a freight train while you're doing the dishes, other times it lurks in the shadows of an old bookstore or arises with the dawn chorus. The key is to be open to it, to position your mind like a satellite dish tuned into the frequencies of the universe.

One reliable source? The very patchwork quilt of life itself! Those thrills and spills, heartaches and belly laughs, they're all fodder for the songwriting mill. Reflect on your own experiences, dive into the pool of your emotions. Whether it's a song whispering out of a moment of joy, or a powerful ballad born from sorrow, your life is a treasure trove of lyrical gems.

Let's not forget the grand tapestry of nature. Ever stood on a cliff edge, felt the sea spray on your face, and the majesty of the landscape stretching out before you? That enormity, that sense of being a small part in something vast—it stirs the soup of creativity. It's in the rustle of leaves, the rhythm of the waves. Get yourself out there, and listen.

And what about the people around us? Talk to an old soul who's lived a nine-act drama or listen to the bubbling enthusiasm of a child. People are walking stories; you just need to be willing to ask them for a chapter or two. Sometimes, the simple act of conversation illuminates a slice of life you never considered, and that flicker of understanding can light a creative fire.

Books, films, and art, oh my! These are the bountiful harvests planted by creatives before us. When you witness another person's creativity, it's like standing on the shoulders of giants. You see further, think wider, and dream in Technicolor. Plunge into these worlds created by others and let their ideas prompt your own.

Music, needless to say, is an archive of emotions made audible. Listen widely and wildly. Let the bravado of a rock anthem, the sultry mood of a jazz saxophone, or the plaintive warble of a country fiddle stir something in you. New genres might not be your cup of tea at first sip, but they hold different keys for unlocking new doors in your mind's corridor.

Travel, too, can be a faithful muse. A change of scenery has the power to topple writer's block like a house of cards. The pulsing beat of a city, the tranquil murmur of a village, or the otherworldly silence of a desert—each has its own rhythm and cadence that can march straight into your compositions.

Even stillness and solitude can be your allies. In the quiet moments, when the constant hum of life subsides, your inner voice becomes audible. This is your raw, unedited self. Allow these quiet moments to ferment; sometimes it's from this silence that the loudest ideas can emerge.

Don't overlook memories either. They may be colored by nostalgia or sharpened by clarity; either way, they are your history set to melody.

Sifting through the annals of your life can reveal forgotten tales itching to be spun into song.

But beware, waiting for inspiration to strike can be like waiting for rain in a drought. It's a surefire route to frustration. Instead, imagine yourself as a miner, chipping away daily in the caverns of creativity. Set up routines that summon your muse, because inspiration loves to catch you hard at work—as the saying goes, fortune favours the prepared.

It's also about keeping yourself primed and ready. Carry a notebook, use your phone, hum into a recorder. When a ghost of a melody or a whisper of a lyric comes to you, snatch it from the air and pin it down. You never know which fragment might grow into a full-fledged song.

In essence, inspiration is a wild beast roaming the landscapes of existence, but it often leaves tracks for those who are willing to embark on the hunt. So keep your well of inspiration brimming by seeking novelty and experience, and don't forget to keep your inner wellspring unblocked and free-flowing.

One final piece of sage advice—don't get too hung up on the search. Let inspiration know you're seeking it, but not that you're desperate. Desperation has a funny scent that can send the muse scurrying. Instead, remain open, stay curious, and, above all, keep your heart poised on the edge of wonderment.

With every step you take in this life, remember that your unique lens is what casts common sights in new light, setting your songs apart from the chorus of the world. So grab your life by the verses, and let inspiration see you making waves—it'll want to ride along.

Chapter 3:
The Building Blocks of Melody

Just as a master chef knows that a pinch of salt goes a long way, you'll learn that a few well-chosen notes can make a melody stick like sweet honey on the mind's hive. Melody is the sweet siren that calls to your listeners, enticing them into your sonic world. It's a dance of pitches arranged in time, and it's where your song often first says 'hello' to the world. As we delve into the fabric of melody, we'll discover that it's not just a random toss of notes but a thoughtfully stitched quilt that warms the soul. It's about tension and release, the peaks and the troughs, and all the little turns in between. Crafting that hummable tune takes more than just plucking notes from thin air; it's about understanding how these notes talk to each other, knowing when to let them fly and when to reign them in. So, are you ready to weave some melodic magic? Let the symphony in your heart guide you because, within the realm of melodic construction, your inner voice is the finest instrument you have.

Understanding Melodic Structure — now, there's a journey worth taking. Let's unravel this mystery together, step by musical step. As we've already discussed, melodies are the spine of any song, the part that often lingers on long after the last note has died away. But what makes a melody stick?

Melody, in its most elemental form, is a series of musical notes arranged in a specific sequence that holds meaning and evokes emotion. Imagine it as your favourite book; the notes are akin to words, and the melodies are sentences that tell the tale. To understand a melodic structure is to become fluent in the language of music, capable of crafting phrases that will resonate with listeners.

The journey of a melody begins with a single note, a point of departure. From there, it travels – ascending, descending, and sometimes pausing for a moment of reflection. A melodic phrase might leap boldly from one pitch to another, or it may step timidly, producing patterns that the ear recognises and the mind remembers.

Repetition plays a crucial role in this dance. Just as a poem has a refrain, melodies often have recurring motifs or themes. Think of these as anchor points within the chaos of sound, giving a sense of structure and familiarity that listeners instinctively seek. Repetition breeds recognition; recognition breeds connection.

But what is salt without pepper, joy without sorrow? Variation, my friends, is the spice of melody. A repeated line can only stay fresh if contrasted against the backdrop of divergence. Too sweet a song without a hint of bitterness can be cloying. It is the twists and the turns, the unexpected detours, that inject life into a melodic line.

Consider the scales as your palette, an array of colours waiting to paint emotions into being. Each scale sets the mood, with the major radiating joy and the minor shrouding in melancholy. Yet, within those frameworks, countless hues can be created through the blend and shade of intervals – the space between notes – and the rhythm with which they're delivered.

Motion, my dear songsmith, is the essence of melody. A melody must move; it must evolve or risk being forgotten in the hustle of daily life. A great melody tells a story through its motion, a narrative that rises with each climax and falls with every resolution, guiding the listener through a soundscape that only you, the composer, can envision.

Arcs and contours of your melody mirror the human voice. There's a reason why those soaring choruses tug at our heartstrings – they mimic the natural ebb and flow of our own speech. So, when building your melody, let it breathe, sing through it, for it must feel as natural as a conversation with an old friend.

If repetition is the skeleton and variation the flesh of melody, then rhythm is surely its beating heart. The pulse of your piece dictates the pace at which the melody is experienced. A brisk, syncopated rhythm may ignite excitement, while a languid, steady beat might soothe the weary soul. Just remember: the rhythm and your melodic notes should embrace in a beautiful dance. One should not overshadow the other.

Context is king, and even the most exquisite melody can be lost without the right sonic backdrop. As we delve deeper into the realms of harmony and chord progressions in later chapters, keep in mind that a melody must hold its own yet also coexist harmoniously with the chords that support it. A judicious pairing can elevate a simple tune to an anthem that stands the test of time.

So, we build melodic structures not just with notes, but with anticipation and release. The listener yearns for closure, for the final note that brings the journey home. Strategically placed leaps and falls within your melodic line can create tension, longing, the need for resolution which, when delivered, can be deeply satisfying. It's the pay-off of musical storytelling.

Putting pen to paper and trial by sound are the bedrocks of understanding melodic structure. There's theory, yes, but the true comprehension comes from doing. You will fumble, you will hit walls, and sometimes your melodies may not soar as you'd hoped. But each attempt is a step forward on your path to fluency in the language of melody.

Melodic structure speaks of the cultural ties that bind us, the universal language of music that transcends borders. Embrace the folk melodies of our past, the classical motifs that have endured, and the pop hooks that define generations. Draw inspiration from the tapestry of music history – each thread a lesson in melodic wisdom.

Let's not forget that the joy of songwriting is in the exploration. A melody can be as complex as a symphony or as simple as a child's lullaby. The beauty lies not in complexity but in expression. As you craft your melodic structures, let your inner voice sing loud and clear. Let sincerity be your guide, and your melodies will surely resonate.

As we close this chapter, know that crafting a memorable melody is a marriage of technique and instinct, of knowing the rules and when to let your heart break them. So, take what you've learned, play with purpose, and let each note find its rightful place in the melody that you – and you alone – were meant to create. The world awaits your song.

Crafting Memorable Melodies is an adventure—a melodious quest where you're both the hero and the bard, threading notes into a tapestry that will wrap listeners in an embrace of sound. Now, you may think, "Sure, easier said than done." And you're right—that's why we're about to dive into the heart of melody making, spinning threads that stick with you long after the song ends.

To craft a melody that lingers on the lips and flutters in the minds of your audience, you've got to start with understanding what makes a tune 'catchy.' Some melodies are as infectious as laughter in a silent room; they have rhythm, they ebb and flow, they rise and fall. Most importantly, they connect with us on a human level, coaxing out emotions we didn't know were waiting for release.

A memorable melody often begins with simplicity. Think about it—some of the most hummed tunes are the ones that can be played with a single finger on a piano. They don't overcomplicate things; they invite us in. A nursery rhyme complexity, as I like to call it, doesn't mean childish—it means it's accessible.

Yet, where is the fine line between simple and uninspired? The key lies in the unexpected twists and turns. A note dropped here, a half-step bent there, or a rhythmatic hiccup can take a plain series of notes and drape it in intrigue. It's like adding a secret ingredient to a recipe—the small touch that gives it that 'mmh' factor.

Composition is part storytelling, and your melody is the voice of your song's character. It should have emotion baked into every bar. Think of the swell of strings in a dramatic film score as the protagonist comes to a revelation, or the haunting minimalism of a piano piece reflecting solitude. How does the melody make you feel? Aim to invoke those feelings through the musical choices you make.

Repetition is a cornerstone of catchy melodies. It gives our brains a pattern to hold onto, something to expect. But there's a balance—too much and you risk sounding monotonous. Instead, introduce variations. Cascade down a scale on the second go-around, or jump to an octave above on the third. Keep the listener engaged by playing a game of expectation and surprise.

While creating these earworms, don't ignore the rest of your toolkit. Dynamics play a pivotal role in how a melody is perceived. A softly whispered melody can be just as powerful as a bombastic, belt-it-out chorus, depending on how it's used. Dynamics shape the emotional landscape of your piece and can make a simple melody feel complex.

Connecting with your melody means getting to know it intimately, playing it over and over, feeling each interval, and understanding its flow. Sometimes this means you need to step away from any other aspects of the song. Let the melody breathe and find its own space before crowding it with chords and rhythms.

And speaking of breathing, the phrasing of your melody should follow the natural patterns of breath—this not only aids vocalists in performing the song but also instills a sense of organic growth within the tune. Where a phrase ends and the next begins can affect the lyrical delivery and the impact of the melody.

Don't forget the importance of context. The same melody can tell different stories depending on the surrounding harmonies. A major key can turn a sorrowful melody sweet, while a minor key can transform a cheerful tune into something foreboding. Experiment with the harmonic context to uncover the different facets of your melody.

Take inspiration from everywhere, but wear it lightly. You want your melody to reflect you, not become a patchwork of your favorite hits. It's fine to let those influences seep through—they're part of your musical DNA. But always be looking for that personal twist that will make your melody your own, something that speaks with your voice.

As you craft your melodies, don't be afraid to break the rules. Music theory is a guide, not a jailer. If a particular note shouldn't technically work but it sounds right to your ear, trust it. Some of the best musical moments come from happy accidents or deliberate rule-breaking. So lean into those peculiarities—they might just be what makes your melody memorable.

Collaboration can be a boon to melody-crafting. Two heads are often better than one, and an outside perspective might suggest a direction you'd never considered. Share your melodic ideas with others, gather feedback, and be open to evolution. The push and pull between collaborators can give birth to a tune that's resilient and robust.

And when inspiration seems as distant as a star in a cloudy night sky, remember patience is your ally. Melodies can be elusive. Sometimes, like a shy creature in the wild, they need time to emerge from hiding. Work on something else, take a walk, let your mind wander. Often, when you're not trying so hard to catch the tune, it lands softly on your shoulder.

Ultimately, the essence of crafting memorable melodies is understanding that they are the soul of your song. A persistent, compelling melody is a bridge between the heart of the songwriter and the heart of the listener. So, wield your notes wisely, sprinkle them with passion, and don't be afraid to let them soar or whisper, as the song requires. With these melodies, we make more than music—we forge connections that can echo through time and space.

Chapter 4:
Harmony and Chord Progressions

If melody is the soaring eagle in your songwriting sky, then harmony is the wind beneath its wings. It's what turns a line of notes into a cushion of sound that could either give your listeners goosebumps or the sudden urge to grab someone for an impromptu slow dance. In this chapter, we're diving into the beating heart of music: harmony and those oh-so-vital chord progressions. Imagine if you will, each chord as a step on a staircase. You've got to place them in such a way that your climb feels like an adventure; sometimes predictable, other times surprising, but always compelling. We're piloting this ship together through the sweet and stormy waters of major and minor, without getting tangled up in augmented or diminished just yet—that's a journey for another day. You're about to learn how to build chord progressions that not only complement your melodies but also tell stories all by themselves. So, let's roll up those sleeves and start weaving the harmonic tapestry that can make your next tune feel like home—or an expedition to parts unknown.

The Role of Harmony in Songwriting We're waltzing into the world of harmony, that invisible force that can make your track snap, crackle and pop - emotionally speaking, of course. In songwriting, the harmony isn't simply the backdrop of cords strung together like Christmas lights; it's the emotional soundscape that dictates the sway of your listeners' feelings. It's the unsung hero of musical composition, adding depth and color to your melodic ideas.

Now, imagine a world where your melody saunters through the streets, whether in major scale metropolitans or minor-key alleyways. The buildings it passes - chord progressions, they're called - make the journey intriguing, marking each turn with a feeling, a change in the atmosphere. Harmony in songwriting does just that; it brings context, compliments the melody and sometimes, is bold enough to take the lead and flip the script.

We might think of harmony like the spices in a stew – a pinch of this or a dash of that can enhance flavours or create a completely different culinary experience. In a song, the right chord can sweeten a moment or introduce a pinch of sadness in an otherwise upbeat tune, transforming the listener's experience in a heartbeat.

One could argue that a melody is capable of standing on its own, strutting down melodies lane without a care in the world. Yet, without the rich context harmony provides, could it ever truly resonate with the depth we often crave in music? A solitary voice singing might touch hearts, but add in harmonics that cradle and support it, and you might just have the recipe for a tear-jerker or a soul-stirrer.

Harmony is more than a supporting role; it's the narrative tool in the songwriter's toolkit. And what a mighty tool it is! It can transform a musical space, take us from the club to the cathedral, from a sunlit field to a murky underwater landscape. When we flip through the annals of history, we find songs that have stood the test of time, often those with harmonic backbones that speak to our very souls.

Think of your favorite song, the one that gives you chills or warms you faster than a cuppa in the dead of winter. Now, peel back the melody and listen to the harmony. Notice the way the chords meld, creating tension and release, playing with your emotions as if they were the strings of a harp. Masterful, isn't it?

For the budding songwriter, diving into harmony can be akin to opening Pandora's Box. It's vast, complex, but inventing within this space brings a sense of power, the ability to guide the emotional journey of your audience. You're the captain charting a course through the waters of sound, and it's the harmonic waves that will carry your ship to its destination. Get it right, and your listeners will sail smoothly; get it wrong, and you'll all be in for choppy seas.

The interplay of harmony and melody is like a dance, intimate and intricate. They lean on each other, push and pull, and when in sync, they glide across the dance floor of the listener's conscience effortlessly. It needs both spontaneous intuition and calculated thought. Sometimes, harmony follows the melody, echoing its sentiments. Other times, it leads, pulling the melody into uncharted territories, coaxing it into a new emotional state.

To embed harmony into your songwriting, you don't need to be a maestro. You just need to tune into the emotional core of your music. What's the story you're aiming to tell? Is it joyous? Melancholic? Tranquil or tumultuous? The chords you choose should align with these moods, speaking in sonic hues that paint your song with the appropriate emotional palette.

But remember, there's a fine line between intelligent harmony and a cacophony of sound. Dissonance has its place, but knowing when to resolve it, when to bring your audience back to a familiar sonic home, is key. They say tension and release are one aspect of life, don't they? That push and pull, it's mirrored in our chords, our progressions, our songwriting. It's the heartbeat of our tunes.

Embrace the experimentation that harmony invites. Try walking a chord progression down a path less trodden, stepping outside the tried and true I-IV-V and into the wild unknowns of modal mixture or chromatic wanderings. You may stumble upon a rare flower, a new harmony that speaks in an alluring dialect, ready to enchant your listeners.

All in all, the role of harmony in songwriting is to infuse your music with vivid imagination, to broaden the emotional spectrum of your songs, and to guide your listeners through a storyline without uttering a single word. In essence, it is the glow to your melody's shine, the shadow to its light. Now, go forth and color your songs with harmonic richness – play, explore, and emerge with something that makes your heart sing and your soul dance.

As you venture further into the craft, you might discover that harmony, indeed, is that gentle whisper to the shout, that knowing glance to the outspoken declaration. It's harmony that often says more in its quietude than any roaring chorus ever could. It's the glue of our musical universe, binding melodies to the reality of our emotions, making listeners feel understood and songs feel complete. Embrace its power, and watch as your songs transform from mere collections of notes to experiences that leave your listeners longing for more.

And so, tuning the strings of harmony, plucking at them with purpose, subtlety and verve, the songwriter becomes not just a composer, but a conjurer of feelings. A magician dealing in the currency of chordal alchemy, conjuring up moods and moments that resonate deep within the souls of those who listen. Ain't that the kind of sorcery everyone wishes they could wield?

Crafting Chord Progressions is a journey akin to building a house—from laying down solid foundations to adding those unique decorative touches that make it a home. As we delve into this foundational element of songwriting, we're not just throwing chords together like a salad. Oh no, we're sculpting a harmonic narrative, a soulful sojourn that tangos with our melodies and underpins our lyrical poetry.

Let's kick things off with a whisper of candid truth—we're all friends here. Chord progressions are the scaffolding upon which your song hangs its hat. You can have a melody that soars higher than an eagle, but if your chord progression doesn't have that sturdy structure, well, you might just find your song flapping about listlessly.

Now, I hear you ask, "But where do I start?" Begin with the basics, and that, my melodious companions, is understanding the key your song will reside in. Settle into that key, get cozy, pour it a cup of tea, because it's about to become your home base. Major for that jolly, skip-in-your-step vibe; minor for when your heart's draped in bluesy shadows.

Next up, we anchor down with the tonic, the root chord that gives your key its name. Whether it's in the joyful realm of C Major or the somber echoes of A minor, that tonic is your North Star. Follow it faithfully, and you won't lose your way.

After setting your sights on the tonic, let's tango with chord functions, shall we? Tonic, subdominant, and dominant—the holy trinity of harmonic roles that bind Western music. They're your road map, the wise elders that have guided many a songsmith.

A progression isn't just a random walk in a harmonic park; there's a method to the madness. A dash of tension here, a sprinkle of release there, and suddenly you've got a progression that's all the more enticing. Cadences, those harmonic full stops, can be perfect, imperfect, plagal, or deceptive, and they'll dictate the mood like the weather dictates your choice of hat.

Moving on, I must acquaint you with progressions that have stood the test of time. The timeless love affair between I-IV-V, for example, is a romance that has birthed a thousand tunes. The I-V-vi-IV? Now that's a recipe for a hit, a delightful loop that has underpinned anthems that echo through stadiums.

But let's not rest on our laurels, because repetition might be safe, but innovation is exhilarating. Mixing modes might just be your ticket to a smorgasbord of aural delight. Dabble in dorian, make merry in mixolydian, and your progressions might just sparkle with newfound magic.

Contrary motion and voice leading—don't let the terms intimidate you, they're friends, not foes. They help your chords flow smoothly, like guests gliding gracefully across a polished dancefloor. Each note in the chord has a journey, and these concepts ensure they don't step on each other's toes.

Borrowed chords are like those unexpected guests that pop by to add intrigue to your party. A bit of modal interchange brings richness to your harmonic story, adding layers, depth, and sometimes a much-needed plot twist when the story starts to sag.

Now, venture we must into the land of secondary dominants, those dashing rogues that offer a fleeting change of scenery before whisking you back home. They create a pull, an anticipation, a longing in your soul that only resolution can satisfy.

Let's not forget the subtle charm of suspended chords that leave you feeling like you're hanging mid-air, wishing, hoping, before gently letting you land on terra firma. They tease tension into the mix, heightening that sweet sense of narrative in your harmonic tale.

It's worth noting that simplicity can be powerful. Resist the urge to cluster your song with chordal complexity if the atmosphere calls for placidity. A simple triad can sometimes shout louder than a cluster of sevenths, ninths, and augmented contours. Trust the spirit of your song; sometimes, less is indeed more.

As we come to a close on this session of harmonic alchemy, remember that progressions are your palimpsest—they can be rewritten, reshaped, and reinvented. Keep an open heart to the oldies, but let your soul yearn for the undiscovered, the unwritten symphonies that lie in waiting.

Stay curious, stay bold, and most importantly, stay true to your own voice. Your chord progressions are the rhythm of your inner seas, and when they're crafted with love and intention, they become the unsung poetry that resonates within the souls of those who listen. So go forth, let the harmonies unfold, and may your songs resound with the echoes of your unique universe.

Chapter 5:
Rhythm and Groove

In the symphony that is a song, if melody is the heart, then rhythm is the pulse that makes it spring to life. So, let's groove into the world of beats and bars; where the cadence of a kick drum or the syncopation of a snare can move feet and stir souls. In this chapter, we're gonna dig deep into the very essence of *rhythm*—the skeletal structure on which a song hangs its flesh. We'll explore how it's not just about the consistent tick of a metronome, but the swagger and sway tucked between the lines. Then we proceed to tackle the elusive beast we call **groove**, an enigma wrapped in a riddle, surrounded by a funky beat. It's that intangible magic that commands hips to sway and heads to nod; a phenomenon that captivates and compels without a word uttered. We're diving into the nitty-gritty of developing that irresistible feel which transforms a good song into a timeless, toe-tapping experience. By the end of this rhythmic rendezvous, you'll be equipped to craft grooves that resonate and endure, echoing through time like the heartbeats of giants in the pantheon of musical legends.

Rhythm as the Backbone of a Song - it's the very pulse that your feet tap to, the invisible thread that sews your listeners to the groove. Picture this: you're crafting a tapestry of sound, and rhythm is that strong, steady warp thread that anchors every weft thread - your melody, harmony, lyrics, and all.

Rhythm isn't just about the beats per minute; it's the way those beats are presented - the pattern, the emphasis, the space. It's the bossy boots that tells the other musical elements when to strut and when to linger. If you're conjuring up a tune and overlooking rhythm, mate, you're on a rowboat with no oars.

When we think of rhythm in the context of our beloved songs, we think of the drum patterns, the subtle slap of the bass strings, the rhythmic strumming or picking on the guitar. Every instrument, including the very cadence of the human voice, contributes to this dance of timing and emphasis.

So, what gives rhythm its thumping supremacy? Dynamics, baby! Rhythm thrives on the varying intensity of notes. It means understanding the difference between pounding your foot down on the pedal and gently tapping the brake. Dynamics and rhythm work together like a charm to keep the listeners engaged and excited.

Syncopation is another little trick – it's the rhythm's cheeky way of catching you off guard with unexpected accents. It's the spice that can turn a generic patter into a compelling foot-tapper. A little syncopation can give your song that hip-swaying, head-nodding vibe that people just can't resist.

You might've heard about time signatures – they're the blueprint, the plan of the rhythmic house you're building. Whether you're working in common 4/4 time or waltzing through a 3/4, it's the time signature that outlines the basic structure of your song's rhythm.

Then there's tempo – the speedometer of your song. The tempo sets the mood – a melancholic ballad saunters slowly at a languid pace, while a jubilant pop anthem gallops at full tilt. Remember, the tempo is your song's heartbeat, so monitor it closely and adjust accordingly to the life you want to breathe into your song.

But how do we 'feel' rhythm?—it has to be more than just counting beats. That's where the groove comes in. Groove is rhythm's irresistible cousin that no one can ignore—it makes the rhythm breathe, swagger, and resonate with the body's instinctive movements.

In some mystical way, rhythm connects with our primal instincts—it's the part of music people respond to, even if they can't carry a tune or recall lyrics. That's why when your baseline for rhythm in songwriting is rock solid, everything else can be built upon it more easily. It's the foundation upon which the house of melody, harmony, and lyrics stand proudly.

Don't forget, subverting rhythm can be just as powerful as following it. Sometimes, playing with the absence of rhythm, or inserting a rest where the ear expects a beat, can create a dramatic effect that heightens the impact of the song. It's all about the expectation, the pause, the surprise!

Rhythm complexity varies too. Some genres, like funk or Latin, demand intricate polyrhythms that can seem overwhelming at first. But fear not; like any great skill, it comes with time and practice. Start simple, master the basics, and before you know it, you'll be the puppet master of those rhythm strings, making them dance to your whims!

A great way to get to grips with rhythm is to listen - not just passively, but actively. Dissect your favorite tunes, tap out their rhythm, and try to understand their underpinnings. How does the rhythm change throughout the song? What makes the rhythm in the chorus so infectious compared to the verse? These insights are like gold dust for your own songwriting journey.

Even the words you choose in your lyrics can play into the rhythm—their syllables can march along with the beat, or skip and tumble over it. Remember, in music every element has rhythm, whether it's the lingering hold of a note or the rapid-fire delivery of a rap verse.

Lastly, don't just think, feel. When you play with rhythm, let it move through you. Close your eyes and let the rhythm guide your body. If you understand it on this visceral level, you'll find it easier to translate it into your songwriting in a way that'll get others moving too.

Rhythm, in all its multifaceted glory, truly is the backbone of a song. So nurture it, challenge it, play with it. Give it the reverent focus it deserves, and you'll arm yourself with the power to turn a humdrum tune into a rhythm-rich anthem that none can forget. Let it be the sturdy foundation upon which your musical dreams can soar!

Developing Groove and Feel in songwriting isn't just about hitting the right notes or strumming in time; it's about creating a heartbeat for your track, something that listeners can't help but move to. It's that infectious pulse, the undercurrent that carries the music forward. Whether it's a smooth, sultry ballad or a funky, upbeat dance number, the groove encapsulates the song's essence, transforming it from a mere sequence of notes into an experience.

Imagine the last time your foot started tapping without thought, or that head-nod that came on as if by instinct. That, my friend, is the secret sauce of groove. To infuse your song with feel, consider the nuances of timing. Don't just play on the beat – play around with it. Pushing slightly ahead of the beat can inject energy, while hanging back a touch can lay back in the pocket. This ebb and flow of time is what gives music its lively, breathing quality.

Dynamics are your best friend here. They're what makes the whispering hi-hat stand out against a thunderous bass drum. It's the soft pluck of the guitar string before the crescendo of a mighty chorus. Dynamics shape the feel, delineating the verses from the bridges and the hooks. Play around with volume, and you play around with emotion, beckoning the listener into your musical world.

Texture plays a significant role in developing groove and feel. A sleek, silky texture lends a different vibe than a gritty, distorted one. By varying the textures within a song, you create landscapes of groove, each with its own unique contour and flavor. The contrast between smooth verses and a gritty chorus can make the latter hit with unexpected gravit.y

Don't forget the silence, for it is in the space between the notes that rhythm blooms and groove emerges. Silence can be as powerful as sound, offering respite, creating suspense or simply giving the groove space to breathe. It's in the breaks, the rests, and the held breath before the beat drops that the feel of a song often truly comes alive.

Syncopation is another critical tool. By emphasizing the off-beats, or the weaker beats in the bar, you can make a rhythm more interesting, compelling, and danceable. It introduces an element of surprise and encourages the body to move in new ways. It's the unexpected bounce that gives a groove its playful character.

Instrumentation also has a huge impact on groove. The choice between a shaker or tambourine, fretless bass or slap bass, can significantly alter the rhythmic feel of a piece. Experiment with different instruments - traditional and unconventional alike - to find just the right timbre and rhythmic character to underline your song's groove.

Interaction between the instruments is the dance within the dance. It's about the bass conversing with the kick drum, the rhythmic dialogue between guitar and piano, or the way the backbeat on the snare talks to the lead vocal. When instruments lock in with each other, they forge a feel that's coherent, compelling, and irresistibly groovy.

Beyond the technical aspects, groove requires a certain attitude. It takes confidence to lay down a line with certainty and finesse. Don't be afraid to take risks and commit to your rhythmic decisions. Groove should exude an aura; it's the way you say, "This is how the song moves, and you're coming along for the ride".

Listen to the groove maestros—those songs and artists you can't resist swaying to. Analyse what they do, how their rhythms breathe, how they shape dynamics or texture to create an unmistakable feel. Take those lessons and apply them to your music. Dissecting what makes other songs groove will help you sprinkle a little stardust on your own rhythms.

Practice is indispensable; groove is a language, and like any language, fluency comes with immersion. Spend time jamming along to different tracks, genres, and rhythms. Feel the pulse of reggae, the swagger of blues, the precision of funk. Each time you play along, you're absorbing new elements of feel, rhythm, and style.

Recording yourself can be incredibly instructive. Often what we feel we're playing isn't exactly what lands on the recording. Listen back critically and hone in on where your groove shines and where it could use some tightening up. The tape doesn't lie, and it can be one of your most valuable teachers.

Lastly, collaboration with other musicians can elevate your sense of groove. Rhythmic ideas can bounce back and forth, forging grooves that might not have been found alone. Each player brings a unique feel and rhythm to the table, meshing their personal grooves to create something richer and more robust.

Embrace the imperfections too. Sometimes it's the slight variations, the human discrepancies from absolute timing, that breathe the most life into a groove. Don't sanitize your tracks trying to chase mechanical precision—feel is found in the humanity of music, in the realness of its rhythm.

Groove and feel are what make your song resonate on a primal level. They invite movement, expression, and an intrinsic connection to the music. When you find the right groove for your song, it doesn't just complement the melody and lyrics; it elevates the whole composition into something that pulses with life. Just remember, the groove is in you; your job is to let it out.

Chapter 6:
Lyricism and Storytelling

Stepping into the realm of lyricism and storytelling is like wading into the warm, sparkling waters of a sunlit sea—it's where the soul of your song starts to swim. This chapter is your dive-in point, where you'll learn that words aren't just words when they're cradled by a melody; they're the heartbeat of your song's story. Throw away the notion that your lyrics have to be a cryptic puzzle only a genius could solve. Simplify. Say it straight, say it slant, but say it true. Here, we'll slip into the shoes of your listeners and explore how the perfect blend of narrative and rhyme weaves the kind of magic that has audiences hanging on every word. We'll delve into the craftsmanship behind the lyrics that stick like honey on the mind and paint pictures in the heart. So, let's spin tales that resonate, that shout and whisper, laugh and weep, that speak in metaphors or march ahead in plain speech. It's time for your stories to sing, your verses to dance, and your choruses to echo in the corners of strangers' rooms.

The Power of Lyrics in Song Composition - let's dive into the heart and soul of a song, the lyrics. Okay! So, you're weaving together melodies, harmonies, and rhythms; but, my friend, have you really tapped into the mighty force of words? Lyrics have powers akin to alchemy in music. They can transform simple notes into anthems that tear at the soul or ballads that tenderly cradle the heart.

Think of lyrics as the storytellers in music's enchanting universe. They're not just a string of fancy words; they are the voice of your inner emotions, set free to the world. A single well-crafted line can resonate with your listeners, nurturing a connection that goes beyond the confines of time and space. It's like giving your song wings, and buddy, you want those wings to be strong and wide.

When lyrics and melody lock in step, it's like a dance – sometimes they waltz, other times they tango, on occasion, they might even do the funky chicken. The point is: the way the words curl around the tune makes your toes tap or can stop you dead in your tracks. That's when you've nailed it – the symbiotic partnership between the beat and the prose.

You see, songs are like whispered secrets shared between strangers on a train. They're intimate. Lyrics provide those hushed tones, that sincerity of sharing something deeply personal in a crowded room, yet only one soul in the corner hears you. There's an art to making your audience feel like that one listening soul.

But let's not forget the technical side. Lyrics need structure; they demand a certain finesse. From verse to chorus, bridge to refrain, the placement of words is a deliberate choice. It impacts the ebb and flow of the storytelling. Master the cadence, understand where to place the emphasis, and you'll have a roadmap that leads the listener through an unforgettable journey.

Metaphors and similes are the spices in your lyrical stew. They add that kick, that unexpected twist of lime that makes your song visceral. But careful there, you don't want to overdo it and leave your audience with heartburn. Great songwriters balance fresh imagery with clear communication. It's about saying what you mean without saying it outright sometimes.

Then there's rhyming, a beast in its own right. Rhymes have the gripping power to catch an ear. They can snap, crackle, pop, or flow like the Ganges. It's our innate love for patterns that drives the appeal of rhyme. But heed this – rhyming for the sake of it is like serving a bland stew; you need the meat, the veggies, the broth to all come together harmoniously.

Don't underestimate the power of repetition, either. It can be the hammer that drives the nail of your message home. A repeated phrase, a motif in lyrics can become the hook that makes the song sticky, glueing it for days in the heads of those who hear it. A cleverly injected line or word repeated can become the battle cry of your song.

Conversely, you must embrace the beauty of brevity. The truth is, sometimes less is indeed more. Think of haiku poets – how they capture the vastness of oceans in a few short lines. Apply that same principle, and watch how a handful of words unlocks a treasure chest of meaning and feeling.

Evoke emotions! The human experience is a rich tapestry of sentiments. The best songs are those that can tap into this deep well. Mix the blues with joy; it's the sweet and sour recipe for soul-stirring tunes. Craft lyrics that can make a listener laugh through tears or shiver though it's not cold. Touch upon hope, pain, love, loss – celebrate them, mourn them, shake hands with them in your lyrics, and let them come alive.

But, what about the darker side of life? Ah, don't shy away from it. Some of the most profound lyrics are born from the shadows. Just remember to hold a light – even the saddest of stories can be told with a tone of healing or revelation. Explore the depths, but give your audience the string of Ariadne to find their way out of the labyrinth.

Now, context – let's hammer this one. Lyrics must speak the language of their time and yet aspire to be timeless. It's like capturing lightning in a bottle – you want that electric shock of the 'now' to last long enough so the future can say, 'Hey, I feel that too.'

And if you're wondering about honesty and authenticity – they're the bread and butter of lyric writing. Be raw, be unfiltered, put the marrow of your story into the lyrics. People can smell a forged tale from a mile away; it just doesn't resonate the same as the truth served on a silver platter.

Let's round off with the notion of diversity in lyricism. Don't chain your words to one genre or theme. Let them roam the wild, wide world of ideas. The more you read, experience, and observe, the richer your lyrics will be. There's an entire encyclopedia of emotions out there and your lyrics should strive to be the historian that captures it all.

In conclusion, lyrics are the spark in the night sky of song composition. They're your chance to set the heavens alight with your personal brand of firework. Give them the thought, the care, the craft they deserve, and watch as they illuminate the hearts and minds of those who come across your music. After all, in the grand theatre of songwriting, the lyrics are the script from which every melody acts, every beat moves, and through which, ultimately, your musical story is told.

Techniques for Effective Storytelling in the world of songwriting invite you to weave narratives that resonate with souls and toe-tap to their heartbeat. So let's dive into the heart and howl of storytelling, where the notes play as much a part as the words.

First up, one must recognise that storytelling through song is a mighty river that ebbs and flows with emotion. The trick is to dip your pen into this river and let the current guide the tale. Yes, it's that blend of the instinctual with the deliberate that births a story listeners will carry in their chest long after the final chord fades.

Now, folks often ask, "How do you start?" Begin with a single, striking image—a moment frozen in time, an emotion that claws at your insides. It's this imagery that paints the scene for your audience, an invitation to step into another's shoes, or dance in another's soul. Keep your imagery sharp, my friends, a beacon to guide through the mist of human experience.

Let's talk about characters. See, a song without a soul is like a drum with no rhythm – it just won't jive. Your characters breathe life into your story, and they don't need to be complicated to be compelling. A few well-chosen words can sketch a character that feels like an old friend - or a mysterious stranger.

Conflict, my melodic compatriots, is 'the' spice in your storytelling curry. Without it, you're just serving plain rice. Conflict gives your story stakes, propelling it from humble beginnings to a crescendo of resolution, or sometimes delicious, poignant ambiguity.

Ah, perspective – the window through which we spy on our musical narrative. Whether you're crooning in the first-person or narrating from a lofty third, your choice of perspective is key. It shapes the intimacy of your story, deciding whether we're sipping tea with the protagonist or watching their world from a cloud.

Now, what about structure? Verse, chorus, bridge – they're not just parts of your song; they're chapters in your narrative. Craft each section with intent, my tuneful tale-tellers, for they must rise and fall like the tides, guiding listeners through the ebb and flow of your saga.

Continuity, an often-overlooked spice in the storytelling gumbo, ensures that your tale doesn't jolt the listener from their reverie. Keep your threads woven tightly, from the keys of your piano to the syllables that linger on your tongue.

Dialogue in songs, now that's a nifty trick. It's like opening a window straight into a scene, letting your audience eavesdrop on reality. Used wisely, it can add authenticity and drive your story forward with a pace that prose cannot always match.

Mood and tone, like the brushstrokes of a painter, tint your song with shades of feeling. Through the choices of chords, tempo, and language, you invite listeners into a world that's sombre, jubilant, contemplative, or wild. Remember, the soundscape you create is as much a part of the story as the tale itself.

Of course, no good yarn is spun without a stitch of transformation. Reflect growth, change, or the lack thereof. Your characters – and perhaps even your listeners – should emerge from the song as altered beings, transformed by the journey of melody and words.

Don't be shackled by the mundane! Metaphors and similes are your linguistic acrobats; they somersault and dance, bringing flair to your storytelling. Injecting these into your lyrics offers a transformative lens through which everyday occurrences shine with the magic of the extraordinary.

The hook or, as I like to call it, the heartstring tugger, is crucial. It isn't just catchy; it encapsulates your narrative's soul. Listeners might forget a verse, trip over a bridge, but the hook is what will haunt them, what they'll hum in the shower or under a canopy of stars.

Juxtaposition, folks – now that's how you craft contrast in a tapestry of sound. Placing love beside loss, hope against despair, not only highlights the richness of human experience but also gives your song narrative depth that can be felt in the old ticker.

And finally, let's not forget the power of silence. A rest, a breath – these moments woven into your melody can speak volumes. They give your audience space to digest the tale, to feel the weight of words left unsaid, and to anticipate the next chord in the grand symphony of your song.

So there you have it, a chorus of techniques to help your stories fly on the wings of song. Each story beat should resonate with the pulse of life, and in doing so, you become more than a songwriter—you become a story weaver, threading tales in the tapestry of sound that echo in the hearts of those who listen. Now, go on and spin your yarns, let them ripple through the airwaves, for a song without a story is a bird without wings—it just can't soar.

Chapter 7:
Song Structures and Forms

Having explored the potent combination of melody, harmony, rhythm, and evocative lyricism, let's talk shop about the architecture of a song. Consider the song structure as a sturdy skeleton that holds the flesh of music and lyrics intact. There's an art to choosing the right frame, be it the ubiquitous verse-chorus-bridge, or perhaps a more freestyle AABA. But it's more than just about sticking to a formula; it's about instinctively knowing how to accentuate the highs and mellow the lows, labelling each section with the kind of purpose that keeps the listener hooked. So, as we dive into the nitty-gritty of song forms, you'll learn to craft a blueprint that best clothes your tune in the fabric of continuity and surprise. It's about painting pictures with progressions and capturing hearts with hooks, all while orchestrating the ebb and flow of musical tensions like a maestro with a baton. Let's unravel the enigma of song structures and learn to tailor them to our sonic narratives – because in the hands of a songsmith, structure isn't constraint, it's the canvas of creativity.

Exploring Different Song Forms Let's dive into the heart of songwriting; the architectural designs that give rise to hits and classics, the song forms. We're talking about more than just verses and choruses here. We're talking about the blueprint of emotions, the skeleton that every musical body depends on to stand tall and proud.

First and foremost, song forms are like recipes. Just as you can whip up a mean chili with varied ingredients and spices, you can cook up a tune with different structures. The most common you'll encounter is the verse-chorus form. This is our meat and potatoes, a comfort food for the listening soul. Your verses set the scene, telling us bits of the story, while that catchy chorus comes in like Sunday roast dinner, filling and familiar, begging you to come back for more.

But don't get too cozy yet. There's also the binary and ternary forms, and no, we're not about to dive into a computer programming manual. Binary, A-B, takes you on a journey from point A, maybe a contemplative verse, to point B, a contrasting section, akin to shifting from a hearty stew to a zesty sorbet. Ternary, A-B-A, brings you full circle, a sonic boomerang that leaves you right where you started, but changed, perhaps, wiser.

Moving into more elaborate territory, we find the rondo form. Think of this as the buffet of song structures. You have your main theme, the A section, and then a variety of contrasting dishes - the B, C, D sections - to sample in between the recurrent servings of A.

The strophic form is simplicity at its best, repetition that hammers home a point, each verse set against the same melody - a powerful tool for storytelling. It's like a poetic chant that mesmerises, hypnotises, and captures the essence of a narrative.

Less common, but thrilling, is the through-composed form. This one's a thrill-seekers' rollercoaster - no repetition, just a continuous stream of musical ideas. It's spontaneous jazz, it's unpredictable storytelling, it's that delightful friend who can't stick to one topic, but captivates you at every turn.

Hang tight, we're not done! The twelve-bar blues isn't just a form; it's a legacy, an institution of songwriting. Built on a repetitive chord progression, it's the backbone of countless classics, a canvas for lyrical and instrumental improvisation.

Is your head spinning yet? Take a breath, and let's consider the ballad form, where you often find a mix of strophic and through-composed tendencies. With a focus on emotive storytelling, the ballad is your heartfelt, tear-jerking, lighters-in-the-air song that reaches deep into the listener's soul.

Now, don't overlook the AABA form, which was the bread and butter of Tin Pan Alley tunesmiths. It's the stuff of 'golden oldies,' built around a memorable hook in the B section, the 'bridge,' offering a refreshing musical and lyrical palette cleanser before returning to the familiar A sections.

There's also the less conventional, but no less creative, palindrome or mirror form. It flirts with symmetry, echoing motifs, and themes forward and backward, creating a sense of unity and closure that can be deeply satisfying to the ear.

Let's not forget about the modern pop song form, where structure sometimes flies out the window for the sake of innovation. Verses and choruses might blur, unexpected bridges can appear, and the notion of a 'hook' is ever more fluid, it's the culinary equivalent of molecular gastronomy in songwriting!

Now, not all songs need to fit neatly into these boxes. The freedom inherent in songwriting allows you to craft hybrid forms, mixing and matching elements as you see fit. Perhaps you start with a strophic model but throw in a contrasting bridge or codetta for that extra spice, creating your own signature dish.

Understanding these forms is not about restricting creativity; it's about giving it a well-defined playground to frolic in. Sometimes, knowing the rules inside out is the very thing that empowers you to break them with flair and purpose.

As you explore, remember that each song form carries with it a weight of expectations. Listeners may not know the technicalities, but they feel them. They anticipate the return of that chorus or the surprise of a bridge. Your job as a songsmith is to balance the comfort of the familiar with the thrill of the new and unexpected.

Ultimately, the song form you choose should serve the song itself. It's about finding the right vessel to carry your melody, lyrics, and emotion to the listener's ears. So, whether you're baking up a classic A-B-A or concocting a zesty through-composed concoction, make sure it's in service to the story you're telling and the feeling you're aiming to evoke. And with that, go forth and play with the forms; let them be your guide, not your cage, as you carve your own path through the wonder-filled process of song creation.

Tailoring Structure to Your Song Now, we're diving into the realm where the rubber meets the road. To craft a song that breathes life into your vision, you gotta know the bones on which your musical flesh hangs, and how to twist and tweak them until they fit the shape of your imagination. We've discussed song forms before, but here we're going to get into the nitty-gritty of making that structure sing for your song.

Picture your favourite song in your mind. Does it start with a bang or does it lure you in with a whisper? That's the kind of choice you're in the driver's seat for. Sometimes, your tune needs to kick off with a verse, setting the stage before the chorus sweeps in. Other times, it demands to start with the chorus, pulling listeners into the deep end right from the get-go. You've got to feel the energy of your song and let that guide your structure.

But what about the bridge, you ask? Sometimes you've got a song that just flows like it's sipping sweet tea on a porch swing, and suddenly, you have to disrupt that rhythm with a bridge that takes your listeners on an unexpected detour. That bridge can be just what you need to spice things up, to elevate the tension before you release it again into the familiar arms of another chorus.

Have you ever thought about how powerful a pre-chorus can be? That climbing anticipation that builds right before your chorus explodes is like the tick of a roller coaster climbing to the top. Don't leave your audience hanging – not every song needs a pre-chorus, but if yours feels like it's missing a stepping stone between verse and chorus, the pre-chorus might be your answer.

Versatility in song structure isn't just about what's there; it's also about what's not. Ever heard a song with no chorus? It's like a stream of consciousness, a cascade of verses that draw you into a narrative without ever handing over that repetitive hook. It's unconventional, sure, but it can be compelling as ever if it suits the story you're telling.

The fabric of your song might call for an instrumental break – space for the music to speak where words just won't suffice. Some emotions are too complex, too rich to be captured in lyrics. In those moments, lead with a sax solo, a guitar riff, or a trippy synthesiser sequence to let your audience feel the vibe.

Reprises are another indulgence you might want to consider. They're like those sneak peeks at the end of a show that bring you full circle, leaving you feeling complete. A reprise can be a lyrical and melodic throwback, a reminder of where you've been and the journey you've taken through the song.

But in all this tailoring, you gotta keep your tape measure handy. Balance is key. Too much padding and your song sags where it should soar. Be critical with your structure – if it ain't adding anything, maybe it's chaff that needs to be cut. Keep your song trim where it needs to be, and give it room to breathe where it yearns for space.

And let's talk about experimentation. Trust your instincts and dare to play with form. The chorus doesn't always have to be after the second verse; it can be the opener, a standalone section, maybe even your entire song. Dive into the unknown and see what treasures you find for your musical puzzle.

As you're shaping and moulding your song, remember that contrast can be your best friend. A subdued verse against a powerful, soaring chorus heightens the impact of both. It's like the ebb and flow of the tide washing over golden sands. Find places where a change in dynamics, rhythm, or melody can serve as contrast, and you'll infuse your song with a captivating push and pull.

An element often overlooked is the outro. Your song's farewell should be crafted with as much care as its hello. Consider a fade-out that leaves your listeners wanting more, or a clear and definitive end that snaps like the finality of a storybook closing. Your outro is the final impression, the last word in your song's conversation with the world.

Remember, too, that silence can be as telling as sound. A well-placed pause within your song structure, a breath between the notes, can give a weight to words and melodies that they may not carry on their own. Sometimes what you don't play says as much as what you do. Use silence to punctuate, to highlight, and to make your listeners lean in closer.

Finally, don't forget to let the theme or message of your song be a compass for its structure. A confused song structure can dilute a potent message. If your story is linear, your structure should probably follow suit. If it's more abstract, fragmented, or circular, let your form mirror that complexity. Your structure should serve as the spine that supports the flesh of your lyrics and melodies, helping to communicate your vision as clearly and powerfully as possible.

But let's not get too bogged down by rules and norms. The songwriting stars didn't always follow the roadmap – they often made their own constellations. Your mission is to be authentic to the song that's bursting from your heart. Try on different structures like outfits; discard the ill-fitting ones and wear the one that feels like it was made for this song and this song alone.

In inking your song into existence, remember it's a living, fluid form. It's a tapestry of your feelings and experiences, woven with threads of melody, harmony, rhythm, and word. Let your intuition guide you, and don't shy away from tearing up the blueprint. Sometimes, it's in the ruins of plans well laid that the true gem of a song is found, gleaming in the rubble, waiting to be discovered by an audience eager for something that resonates with their own tapestry.

Chapter 8:
The Sonic Palette: Instruments and Arrangement

Okay, so you've got your melody, your chords are slick, and your rhythms got that stick-to-your-ribs kind of groove. Now, you're gazing into the wondrous abyss we call the 'sonic palette.' Well, it's time to pick up the brush and start painting with sound! The choice of instruments and their arrangement is much like choosing colors for a canvas – it's all about balance, texture, and contrast that breathe life into your musical masterpiece. We're talking the buttery warmth of a cello undercurrent, the sparkling chatter of a hi-hat, the raw crunch of an overdriven guitar, or the humble honesty of an acoustic strum — each one a thread in the tapestry of your track. How you weave them together? That's the sorcery of arrangement. Get ready to dive deep into the alchemy of figuring out which instruments play what, when, and how they all fit together to tell the story you're aching to share. Matching the emotional weight of your lyrics to the timbre of a piano or the intensity of your beats to the boom of a bass — that's what makes a song leap from mere notes on a page to a living, breathing entity. So, let's get our hands dirty and explore how to use this sonic palette to paint songs that resonate and endure.

Choosing the Right Instruments – Ah, we're delving into the veritable paintbox of songwriting: the instruments. Imagine each instrument as a colour, offering a unique shade and texture to your sonic canvas. Now, the key isn't just to grab every crayon in the box; rather, it's about choosing the right hues that elevate your masterpiece without causing a visual kerfuffle. So, let's simmer down and chat about how we go about picking our musical confidants for composing that hit – or perhaps, that mellow ditty that serenades the soul.

Firstly, consider the heart of your song. What's the beat? Every genre whispers sweet nothings about its preferred instruments; folk might beckon an acoustic guitar while funk is all up on that bass. Decipher the core vibe of your tune and let that guide you towards the instrument family – be it strings, brass, woodwind, percussion, or those digital wonders synthesizers. Each brings a character, a personality that must jive with your song's soul.

Now, let's chat melody. The dominant voice of your musical escapade, where the intrigue, or moreover, the hook of your song lies. Choosing an instrument that sings this element with the right timbre is like choosing the perfect leading actor for a box office hit. Will your melody ride on the silky resonance of a piano, or the raw edge of an electric guitar?

Harmony follows suit, like a best mate ready to back you up. Picking an instrument that provides a lush backdrop or a silky undercurrent can elevate your tune from sounding like a simple sketch to feeling like the Sistine Chapel's ceiling. Think about the guitar's strum against the mellifluous lines of a cello – a harmonic match made in heaven!

Then, let's not underestimate rhythm. What's going to be your timekeeper? Drums, of course, strut their stuff here, but pianos and guitars can also offer rhythmic punctuation that becomes the spine of your song. Even in the digital age, with beat machines aplenty, the choice of rhythm instruments or sampled sounds can take your song to a whole new realm.

When thinking about your song's setting, the overall atmosphere, synth pads or strings to support could be your answer – crafting an ambient cloud where your tune can float and soar. Choosing these layers is akin to a director setting the perfect stage for a big scene; it's all about ambiance and setting the mood.

Let's not forget dynamics, that undulating wave of soft and loud, which breathes life into your composition. An instrument's dynamic range can evoke emotion – a softly played violin can pull at the heartstrings, while a blaring trumpet can rouse a fighting spirit. Choose instruments with the dynamic ability to reflect your song's emotive journey.

Texture, oh sweet texture. An instrument's tone can be as smooth as melted chocolate or as gritty as a gravel road. You must ask – what flavour does your song need? Perhaps a bit of distortion on that guitar for a rock anthem, or a pure, clean piano to compliment a delicate ballad.

Now for those sweet, sweet embellishments – the musical equivalent of a chef's kiss. Instruments like a harp, or perhaps a sprightly mandolin, can add a delightful sprinkle of sonic sparkle that give your song little moments of surprise and delight. These are the dashes of sonic seasoning that make the listener yearn for more.

Expressiveness is yet another facet. Some instruments naturally weep, shout, sigh, and laugh within their sound – yes, they're the drama queens and kings. The deep vibrato of a saxophone may purr with sensuality, while the eloquent articulation of a piano speaks to the intellectual soul. The narrative of your song might just hinge on this choice.

Juxtaposition can be a marvellous game to play – placing classical instruments amongst electronic beats, or a distorted guitar within an orchestral arrangement. This contrast is an invitation to listeners to experience the familiar with a twist, challenging norms and tickling fancies.

Economic considerations also tap on the shoulder. We don't all have the means for a philharmonic backing, do we? Sometimes, invention must be the child of necessity. Embrace the limitations; a minimalist approach with fewer instruments can sometimes tell a story with more clarity and punch than an over-stuffed turkey of a track.

Never forget the technological wonders at our fingertips! Virtual instruments have demolished the gulf between the aspirational and the possible. They offer a smorgasbord of sonic choices without the hefty price tag of a grand orchestra. But remember, with great power comes great responsibility – it's easy to get lost in the vortex of virtuality. Select with the wisdom of a sage.

Practicality chimes in, too. If you're performing live, consider your stage – can the song be replicated in its essence without that army of bagpipers you featured on the track? Maybe rethink that piccolo solo if you can't find a piccolo player, eh?

Finally, trust your instincts. Sometimes an instrument chooses you by the siren call of its sound. At times, it's that almost imperceptible chemistry between the melody and the instrument that can ignite the magic. It's when logic intertwines with intuition that the wizardry happens in music-making.

Choosing the right instruments for your song isn't just science; it's poetry, it's storytelling, it's an art form in itself. It's about weaving a tapestry of sound that captures the mood, enhances the narrative, and ultimately, resonates with the heart. Consider each instrument an ally on your creative quest, a companion on the journey to finding 'that' sound. So go ahead, be the maestro of your own symphony, painting with sound, one note at a time.

Arrangement Techniques for Songwriters Now, let's venture into the realm of arrangement, the unsung hero that can transform your song from a diamond in the rough to a polished jewel. It's like giving your tune a tailor-made suit, ensuring every note fits snugly into its rightful place.

Arrangement is about choices. It's where you decide whether the trumpet takes the lead or the guitar strums the supporting role. It may seem daunting, but with a few choice techniques up your sleeve, you'll soon find your feet tapping along to your own rhythm, creating soundscapes that sing to the soul.

Consider the intro. Do you open with a solo instrument, laying down the red carpet for your vocals? Or do you kick off with an ensemble, making a grand entrance? The beginning of your song sets the tone, invites your listeners into the room, and whispers a hint of the journey they're about to embark on.

Once we're past the intro, we tango with the verse. It's not just about the lyrics; the arrangement here gives them a dance partner. Keep it sparse, let the words breathe, and perhaps introduce new instruments gradually, building layers as the narrative unfolds.

Transitioning to the chorus, that's your moment, the hook, the sing-along bit. Here, thinks big, bold, beautiful. Use harmonies, backing vocals, or a change in the dynamics to elevate the moment. Let it soar, so much so that it imprints on the mind, becoming the part hummed long after the song ends.

And let's not ignore the bridge. This is your curveball, the path less trodden. A change in rhythm, a key shift, or an instrumental solo. It's a scenic detour that brings fresh perspective before you bring us home.

The outro, much like a good dessert, needs to satisfy, rounding off our musical meal. Fade out gracefully or end with a bang? That's your call. Craft it with care to leave that last taste lingering on the listener's palate.

Dynamics are your dial for drama. They draw the listener in close for an intimate whisper or push them back with a wall of sound. Think of dynamics as the heartbeat of your song; they can make a piece pulse with life and command attention.

Variety is the spice, and in arrangement, variation keeps things intriguing. A second verse doesn't have to be a clone of the first. Switch up the beat, play with the bassline, add some stabs of piano or a fluttering flute. Keep your audience on their toes, guessing what delicacy you'll serve up next.

Let's chat about the break, whether it's instrumental or percussive. It's like a brief intermission, giving the audience a moment to digest before diving back in. The break can rejuvenate a song at the right moment, providing contrast and excitement.

Now, instrumentation is your palette of colours. Don't splash them all at once. Start with a few primary hues and blend in more as your song progresses. Each instrument should have its moment, its purpose, not merely there for the sake of inclusion.

Harmony isn't just for choirs. Using backing vocals can add depth and richness to a chorus or highlight key phrases. Just remember, harmony is the support act, enhancing the lead without overshadowing it.

When it's time for a solo, choose your moment and player wisely. A guitar riff, a piano embellishment, or a saxophone wailing into the night – the solo is a spotlight, a narrative within the narrative, a story within the story. Here, musicianship shines brightly, telling its own wordless tale.

Repetition is a necessity, but don't let it become a nuisance. Repeating a riff or a lyrical hook embeds it in memory, but add subtle changes to maintain interest. Sometimes, it's the little things - a shift in the drum pattern, a tweak in the bass groove - that can make a familiar phrase feel fresh again.

In the end, the song's arrangement tells a story as much as its lyrics and melodies. It's the fabric that binds all elements of your song into a coherent, emotive, and captivating narrative. As you hone your craft, you'll grow to appreciate the nuances and the subtleties that arrangement can offer. It's an art, a science, and a little sprinkling of magic that can make your song feel just right.

Chapter 9:
The Songwriting Process:
From Concept to Completion

Swooping down into the heart of song creation, there's a bustling world where ideas flutter and solidify into the marvels we call songs. Here, within the fleshy confines of our musings, we embark on a voyage from the ether of concept to the solid ground of completion. Imagine you're conjuring tunes from the whispers of your soul, blending chords like a wizard from the misty moors—a journey where a single note can start an odyssey. It's a place where workflow isn't just a fancy term, it's your steadfast companion through the labyrinth of melodies and lyric lines.

Whilst wrestling with the beast of procrastination, wrangling with the dragon of doubt, songwriters like you must unsheathe the sword of persistence, crafting and honing your creation with the precision of an artisan. Every verse is a conversation, every bridge a path over tumultuous thoughts, and when that chorus soars, it's like the triumphant bellow of victory. By journey's end, you emerge not just with a song but a testament to your saga—a tale of tuneful conquest from the raw clay of concept to the chiseled statue of completion.

Workflow Strategies for Songwriters

Now, let's dive into the rhythm of creating music, embracing the ebb and flow, the push and pull of the creative process. But how do we harness this rhythm, and what's the best way to steer the ship of songwriting productivity? It's about finding your flow, embracing it, dipping your toes in the stream of creativity and letting the current take you where it may.

The starting point for any songwriter is establishing a routine that plays to your strengths. Maybe you're an early bird, lyrics flowing with the morning coffee, or perhaps the moon is your muse, and midnight strikes a chord within you. Figure out when your mind hums with melodies the most and set that time aside. It's about being consistent, not necessarily about clocking in more hours.

But let's get real, sitting down to write with discipline is simpler said than done. Distractions are a dime a dozen, and procrastination is always lurking. Cue the power of setting the stage – your environment matters! Carve out a creative space, whether it's a corner desk teeming with inspiration or a full-blown studio. Make it a place where inspiration feels at home, and distractions know they ain't welcome.

Okay, so you're in your space, now what? It's time to break down your tasks. Think of it like baking a cake; you don't throw all the ingredients in at once. Start by jotting down lyrical ideas, humming melodies, or strumming chords. Piece by piece, each element of your song will fall into place.

Don't let the blank page intimidate you. Embrace the art of writing rubbish - yes, you heard that right. Sometimes you need to clear the less appealing ideas out of the way to uncover the gems. It's all part of the process. Let your ideas flow unbridled and edit later.

Ever heard of mind maps? They're not just for boardroom strategists. Mapping out your song ideas can visually untangle the threads of your creativity. Connect concepts, lyrics, and melodies in a spider-web of innovation. This technique can offer a fresh perspective and spark new connections in your brain.

Let's chat about setting goals, shall we? No, not the pie-in-the-sky kind. We're talking achievable, bite-sized targets. Writing a whole album in a week? Ambitious, but let's aim for a song or even a verse to keep things real. Goals should motivate, not dishearten.

Technology is your friend, embrace it. There's a galaxy of apps and tools designed to streamline your workflow. Digital audio workstations can make demoes a breeze, while note-taking apps keep those lyrical epiphanies safe. Mix tradition with innovation – a notebook in one hand, a smartphone in the other.

Some days, creativity flows like a mighty river; on others, it's a desert out there. When the latter hits, switch it up. Change instruments, alter your environment, or flip your routine on its head. Often, a simple shift can break the dam and let creativity flood back in.

Collaboration can be the missing piece of the puzzle. Bouncing ideas off another can not only refine your work but can inject a whole new dimension to it. However, remember that every creative partnership should be built on respect and a shared vision for the song's destination.

Reflecting on your work is invaluable. Take a step back, listen to what you've created with fresh ears. Sometimes a break is all it takes for the answer to that tricky bridge to come strolling on in. Reflection fuels refinement, and that's where good songs turn great.

Don't be afraid of criticism. If you've got a circle of trusted peers or mentors, use them. Constructive feedback is the polish your song needs to shine. Take the critique on the chin and use it as a stepping stone to better your craft. Keep your mind open; nobody's perfect, after all.

Lastly, let's circle back to self-care. Burning the candle at both ends can leave your creativity well dry. Ensure you're taking breaks, eating well, and getting enough z's. A well-oiled machine produces the smoothest work – and you, my friend, are a complex, beautiful machine.

Embarking on the songwriting journey is akin to setting sail on a vast ocean. Your workflow strategies are the compass and rudder guiding you through calm waters and stormy seas. Keep your hands steady on the wheel, your eyes on the horizon, and sail on, intrepid songwriter, sail on.

The strategies presented here aim to bestow your toolkit with the finesse of a skilled craftsman. As you chisel away, remember that every song is a stepping stone, each lyric a heartbeat. Care for them, nurture them, and when the time comes, let the world hear the music that has danced within you.

Overcoming Common Obstacles in Songwriting Picture this: you've got a melody that feels like it's caught onto the tail of a comet, and lyrics that could make the stars weep. There's just one snag – you've hit a creative wall, and that comet is starting to feel more like a runaway bus. It happens to the best of us, but don't worry, we're here to get that celestial show back on the road.

First things first, writer's block is as common as rain in London and can dampen the brightest of creative sparks. But here's the thing – it's often just our brain's way of telling us to change up the routine. Try getting out of your usual writing spot. Whether it's your cosy studio or that corner in the cafe where the barista knows your order by heart, switch it up! A change of scenery can work wonders for your creative flow.

Another common hurdle is doubt. Those pesky little thoughts that whisper, "This isn't good enough" or "You can't do this". Well, let me tell you, they're like uninvited guests at your songwriting party. Don't give them any attention. Easier said than done, right? Yet what works is acknowledging them and then pushing through regardless. Remember, every great songwriter has those same doubts; what sets the successful ones apart is they keep writing anyway.

Then, there's the loop of never-ending perfectionism. Striving for excellence is brilliant – it's what makes your work shine. But sanding down a song until it's thin and fragile isn't the goal. Sometimes, a song's beauty lies in its rawness, its authenticity. Perfection is a myth, a mirage in the desert of creativity. Aim for expression, not perfection.

Similarly, finding originality can seem like hunting for a needle in a haystack made entirely of needles – every single one claiming to be the sharpest. Truth is, every story has been told, every chord progression played. The magic lies in your unique perspective. Focus less on being different for the sake of it, and more on being true to your voice. That's where originality naturally flows.

Indeed, there are days when you feel you've run out of things to say, as if the well of inspiration has dried up. This is when you need to go out and live. Experience life, love, heartbreak, joy, boredom – it all feeds into your art. Keep your sense of curiosity alive. Ask questions, listen to stories, soak up the world around you. Inspiration is often where you least expect it.

Lack of structure can also be an obstacle. You start writing with gusto and then... nothing. You don't know where to go next. This is like setting sail without a map. Sure, exploration is exciting, but having a sense of direction is crucial. Familiarise yourself with song structures and forms – they're your maps in the open seas of songwriting. Then, when inspiration strikes, you'll have a framework to pour it into.

What about criticism and negative feedback? Well, any creator who puts their work out there will face it. It's natural to take it to heart, but remember, feedback is like a compass – it shows you where you might need to improve. Take what's helpful, discard what's not, and always stay true to the vision of your song.

Finishing a song can also feel like trying to reach the horizon – it keeps moving away the closer you get. This is often due to a lack of clear goals. Set milestones for your writing. A first draft by Tuesday, a solid chorus by Thursday. Hold yourself accountable, and celebrate small victories – they lead to big ones.

Connections and networking can be daunting. 'Who do I know? Who should I get to know?' These questions can stifle before you even begin. Yet, in this beautiful symphony of life, it's often about whom your music resonates with, not whom you know in the industry. Focus on creating heartfelt work; the right people will tune in to your frequency.

Financial constraints are a reality many face, with high-quality production often seeming out of reach. But in the age of technology, an entire orchestra can live within your laptop. Home recording equipment and software have become affordable and accessible. Use what you have to start creating; refine as you grow.

Distractions are everywhere – social media, chores, that one friend who always calls right when you're about to write a masterpiece. It's crucial to carve out dedicated writing time. Disconnect from the world to connect with your art. Let friends and family know this is your time to create – they'll understand.

If you find yourself struggling with the technical aspects of music theory, remember that it's a tool, not a barrier. Basic knowledge is useful, yes, but many hit songs have come from intuition and feeling rather than textbook theory. Learn the basics, but don't get bogged down. Let your ears guide you.

Lastly, remember that resilience in songwriting is key. Not every day will yield a classic, and that's okay. It's the consistent effort, the day-in, day-out grind, the love for the craft that will ultimately pave the way for success. Keep showing up for your music, and your music will show up for you.

So, there you have it. Obstacles in songwriting are as common as the chords on a guitar, but they're not insurmountable. With a little grit, grace, and a dash of patience, you'll find yourself writing tunes that resonate with the rhythm of life. And always – always – let that creativity flow like a river after the rain. Now, grab your pen, your instrument, and let's create something that makes the heart sing.

Chapter 10:
Collaboration and Co-writing

In the thrilling odyssey of songwriting, joining forces with another creative spirit can be like discovering a new continent in your artistic world. Venture into the realm of collaboration and co-writing, where the fusion of different talents can ignite a burst of new ideas that may never have danced in your head if left to its solitary tango. Imagine the possibility of concocting a chorus richer in harmony because someone else's insight complements your own melodic forays. Yes, it's akin to adding a shot of espresso to your creative process – stimulating, enriching, and sometimes capable of keeping you awake with excitement long into the night! Navigating this co-creative process does mean sharing the steering wheel and sometimes even the backseat. But trust me, it's a journey worth embarking upon. The resulting synergy can lead to a masterpiece that resonates with a wider audience, carries a variety of influences, and showcases a depth that solo efforts might not always reach. When two or more minds with their own quirks and chords come together, the resulting composition can transform from a simple melody into a symphony of collective genius.

The Benefits of Co-writing

Once upon a tune, in the grand medley that is songwriting, there comes a crescendo that can define a career—the mighty collaboration. The art of co-writing, much like a duet in perfect harmony, brings together the individual strengths of songwriters to craft works that resonate with a depth and diversity one voice alone may not deliver. So, let's riff through the wonders that come from melds of musical minds.

Firstly, two heads—or perhaps three, or more—are often better than one. While the solitary songwriter might stumble upon a stumbling block or wrestle with a wicked case of writer's block, the presence of a kindred spirit can cast away those creative cobwebs. Ideas bounce and multiply; what starts as a spark can soon ignite into a burning blaze of innovation.

Moreover, when you co-write, you're tapping into a pool of experiences wider than your own. Lyrics are the soul of a song, and by blending insights and emotions from diverse backgrounds, songs gain a universal appeal. They begin to speak not just to one person's journey but echo the tales of many, and isn't that the very essence of songwriting?

The educational aspect can't be overstated. Working alongside others is like an on-the-spot masterclass. You observe new techniques, perspective-shifts, and workflows. Each session is an opportunity to pick up on the understated intricacies of the craft that could leapfrog your own expertise forward.

Style fusion is another notable perk. Imagine a jazzy groove dovetailing with an indie rock vibe—sounds intriguing, right? Co-writing often results in genre-bending pieces that push boundaries and pave new sonic pathways. These types of collaborations are the petri dishes for the next wave of musical evolution.

And let's talk about the network effect. Your collaborator might have connections in the industry which could prove invaluable. This symbiosis isn't just about crafting a song together; it's about weaving a stronger support fabric for your music career. One that broadens your horizons and could open up possibilities that were previously mere figments of your imagination.

Let's not forget the motivational aspect. A passionate partner will keep you on your toes, challenge you, and maybe even shepherd you through the troughs of disillusionment that occasionally haunt creative endeavours. The mutual commitment to a project may be the just the nudge needed to stride past procrastination.

The joys of co-writing also lie in learning the nuances of conflict resolution and compromise. It's a dance of give and take, where sometimes you lead, and sometimes you follow. Such interpersonal dynamics are not just beneficial for songwriting but for life, infusing a wealth of emotional intelligence into your ventures.

Financially, co-writing can have its merits too. There's potential for revenue sharing, and with more people pushing the song, it stands a better chance in the marketplace. A hit born from collaboration means multiplied returns for all those involved—sweet music to any songwriter's ears.

When we talk about legacy, co-writing can stamp an indelible mark on the canvas of music history. Iconic songs often have multiple creators behind them. These collaborative efforts mean multiple legacies intertwine, allowing your music to live on through various channels long after the last note fades.

Honest feedback is a valuable commodity, and within a co-writing relationship, it's freely given. Fresh ears present constructive criticism, ensuring that the song is polished and honed before it greets its first audience. This iterative process of critique is sanctified ground for any serious songwriter aiming for growth.

Splitting tasks makes for efficient use of time too. Perhaps you're a whiz with words but slow with setting a melody. Co-writing can mean crafting a track in double-quick time with each person focusing on their strengths, turning what could be a laborious solo effort into an inspiringly swift conquest.

On the human level, co-writing begets camaraderie. There's something quite stirring about sharing the act of creation with another soul. It's a bonding experience that engenders a unique companionship, fortified by shared victories and the occasional comforting consolation when things go awry.

Then comes adaptability—a skill honed through the collaboration process. Being receptive to others' ideas, blending different workflows, and navigating the push and pull of creative disagreement, instils a flexibility in your approach to songwriting that stands you in good stead, no matter what project you embark upon next.

Finally, co-writing brings a sense of shared success and joy that simply can't be replicated in solo endeavours. When a song that you've jointly poured your heart into touches someone, the shared pride is doubly sweet. It's akin to a high five that reverberates through the very chords of your being.

In essence, co-writing shapes you into a more robust, versatile, and connected songwriter. It's an exciting avenue filled with potential for both personal growth and professional development. By combining resources, skills, and passions, you're not just penning lyrics and melodies—you're forging the possibility of a legacy that echoes through generations. And isn't that a chorus worth joining?

Navigating the Co-writing Process isn't for the faint-hearted. It's a dance, a dialogue, and sometimes a tug-of-war, but with a bit of wisdom, and a touch of grace, you can weave magic with a fellow troubadour. Collaborative songwriting blends the soulful with the practical. So, let's grope through the murk of mingling muses and learn the ropes together.

First up, your co-writer is not your competition, they're your ally. Treat them as such. Align your weapons – your pens, papers, instruments, and voices – against the shared enemy of mediocrity. Finding common ground is essential. You might come from worlds apart, jazz hands and rock fists, but in the crucible of creation, it's the meeting of styles, sometimes the clash, that kindles the flame of an outstanding song.

Communication is your golden key. If you've got an idea simmering in the depths of your noggin, sing it, hum it, strum it. Let your partner in on the secret symphony in your head. And return the favour. Listen with open ears and a receptive heart to what they bring to the table. Remember, the richest tapestries are woven from diverse threads.

Respect is the sturdy foundation upon which co-writing is built. Songwriting is baring your soul in scribbles and sounds. It's vulnerable business. Honour their offerings as you would your own. If their lyrics don't knock on your heart's door, approach it with sensitivity. 'That's interesting, what if we...' is music to a co-writer's ears when compared to the discordant 'That's not working.'

Compromise, comrades. Neither of you will get their way entirely. That's the beauty of collaboration. Maybe your chorus soars, but their verse grounds it. The push and pull, give and take in the exchange of ideas, that's where the magic often lurks. You're not diluting the potion; you're enriching it with each other's lore.

A touch of structure can keep you from descending into creative anarchy. Set the boundaries – time, space, even subject matter. Decide, is this an hour of brainstorming, or are we on the clock till a full draft is done? Are you the lyricist, and they the melodist? Or will both dip into each realm? Roles can be fluid, but having a clear start boosts productivity.

Now, it's a pickle, but who's the captain of this ship? A gentle hierarchy can keep you off the rocks. It might shift from song to song, but a point person can be a lighthouse, steering your creative vessel through foggy bits. This captaincy isn't about ego; it's about having a go-to decision-maker when you're locked in a stalemate.

Surprise, the unexpected guest at your party—the jazzy chord in a country ramble, the rapped verse in a ballad. Welcome it, hoist it atop your shoulders, and parade it around. The blend of distinct styles, personalities, and experiences can yield unexpected treasures, so be open to the unfamiliar.

Feathers will get ruffled, it's almost inevitable. When that happens, pause and breathe. Take a leaf from the wise oak's book—stand firm but bend before you break. If you need space, state it without making a battlefield of your writing space. Remember, after the storm the sweetest songs are sung.

What about credit, you ask? In the land of the co-write, all should get their due. From the get-go, discuss who did what; a 50-50 split is common, but if it leans more one way, let it be an honest lean. Not talking money and credit is like waltzing on quicksand – charming for a beat, until you're neck-deep with no idea how you got there.

Multi-writer rooms, the symphonies of today. The more the merrier? Perhaps. Still, it's a kettle of fish that needs more hands to stir. Ensure everyone's voice is heard – the shy chord genius in the corner might have the refrain that catapults your song to stardom. Balance input, and keep an eye out to not let one voice override others.

Technology can be our invisible bandmate. Embrace it. Songwriting apps, video calls, online shared workspaces. There's a digital bridge for every physical divide. From sharing demos to real-time collaborative editing, technology can supercharge your co-writing journey and send your songs straddling the globe in search of hearts to captivate.

And if the well goes dry, fear not. Step away. Sometimes the best ideas come when you're not staring each other down across a rhyme-slick battlefield. Take a walk, watch the world—return recharged. The well will fill again; it always does. Your next anthem might just be hiding in the quiet corners of a coffee break.

Finishing a song, now that's a sweet moment. You've toiled, tangled and triumphed. But before you take a bow – edit. Co-writing means co-editing. Attack it with red pens from both sides. Every word, note, and rest must earn its keep. This scrutinising is where good becomes great, where the coal of your efforts is pressed into diamonds.

As you step off the stage of this co-written saga, take heart. You've merged melodies, interwoven inspirations, and created with two souls instead of one. It's not just about the song you've penned; it's the bond of artistic kinship you've forged in the crucible of creation. Take the applause, take a breath, and then, take on the next blank page together.

Chapter 11:
Production and the Home Studio

Now that we've explored the cooperative dance of co-writing, let's venture into the sanctuary of your very own musical haven—the home studio. This is where the magic brews and bubbles, and with a few savvy production techniques tucked under your belt, you'll be crafting sonic gold in no time. Setting up a home studio isn't about breaking the bank; it's about making the space you have work for you, unleashing your songs' potential beyond the scribbled lines on a page. But remember, the goal here isn't to become the next big-time producer overnight. Instead, we're focusing on equipping you with the know-how to give your songs that extra sparkle—from honing a crisp vocal take to laying down a bass line that grooves in the pocket. So, let's roll up our sleeves, fiddle with those knobs, and let the enchantment of music production amplify the stories you're aching to tell.

Basic Production Techniques for Songwriters - Now, you've got this wealth of imagination at your fingertips and a library of tunes swelling in your heart. The time has come to sprinkle a little production magic onto those beautiful ideas of yours. Songwriters, lean in close; let's hatch these melodies into full-blown songs.

Embarking on production can feel just as expansive as staring up at a starry night sky. Where do you even start, you wonder? Well, the first twinkling star in this galaxy of music production is concept realization. Transform that whisper of a tune in your mind into something tangible. Get it down! Whether that's hummed into a voice memo or plucked out on a dusty old piano, capture that idea before it flutters away.

Next comes the assembling of a basic structure — the skeleton if you will. Don't worry about intricate muscle and skin; we're talking bones here. Sketch out your verses, chorus, and perhaps a bridge. Keep it simple, for simplicity is the soil where ingenuity grows.

Once you've nailed down a skeleton, it's time to breathe life into it with a demo. Your recording software, affectionately known as a DAW (Digital Audio Workstation), will be your best friend here. Every songwriter should cozy up to their DAW — it's a sandbox for creativity. Use it to lay down a rough version of your song, playing with different instrument sounds and rhythms.

Exploring the power of a strong, clear vocal can never be underestimated. Even a simple vocal recording, paired with minimalistic accompaniment, can capture the heart of your message. Investing in a decent microphone and learning the ropes of recording vocals will serve you tremendously. Remember, the voice is your most natural instrument; treat it with tenderness and respect.

Now, let's discuss the groove—the heartbeat of your song. A drum loop, a handclap, or even a pencil tapped on a table can lay down the foundation of your rhythm. Flesh out the groove early in the production process; it'll keep the rest of the elements in line, dancing to the same beat.

Chords are the next layer to dress your song. They are the warm woolly jumper wrapping around the spine of your melody. Whether you're a pianist or a guitarist, understanding basic chord progression theory can help structure the harmonic support for your song. Play around with major, minor, and maybe some seventh chords to find the emotional hue you're after.

We move to the bass line — the unsung hero that carries the weight of your track. A bass line doesn't just complement the rhythm;

it marries the harmonic content with the rhythmic drive, creating a richer, fuller sound. The beauty lies in its subtlety and power.

At this juncture, you may be keen to embellish your production with sweeteners. These are the little decorative notes, the ear candies — like a sprinkle of percussion here, a pinch of synthesized texture there. They fill the spaces between the obvious and give your song personality and depth.

Remember that less is often more. This is paramount in song production. You don't want to drown your listener in sound. Instead, guide them through your musical story with clear signposts — a melodic hook, a lyrical phrase, a sudden silence, or a heartfelt harmony.

When the time comes, you'll find mixing is a subtle art all its own. It's where you ensure every element sits comfortably in the sonic living room you've created. Don't let the kick drum hog the couch or the guitars chatter too loudly in the corner. Balance and space will let your song breathe.

Mastering follows mixing and think of it as a final polish on your already shiny song. It's about making sure your creation holds its head up high, no matter where it's played. Whether people listen in their car, on their phones, or with fancy headphones, your song needs to be the best possible version of itself in each scenario.

Finally, my dear creative soul, embrace experimentation in your production endeavor. Be bold. Be brash. Be subtle. Be nuanced. There are no hard and fast rules in this playground. Trust your instincts and your ears; if it sounds right, it probably is.

And don't forget the ultimate test of any song: the vibe check. You know it when a track makes you nod your head or tap your foot without even thinking. That's when you know you're onto something special.

You see, production is more than just a process; it's the canvas for your musical expression. It calls for patience, yes, but also for a heart that's willing to listen. So take these basic techniques, young songsmith, and lay down tracks that ring true to the vibrant songbird within you. Who knows what anthems might rise from these humble beginnings?

Now that we've dipped our toes into the waters of production, rest assured, setting up your own home studio is the next leap forward, and that, my friend, is a story for the following chapter. For now, revel in the magic you create and the soundscapes you sculpt. This is your time. Make every note count.

Setting Up Your Home Studio So, you've got the songs in your heart and the rhythm coursing through your veins. It's time to build that bridge between the melodies in your mind and the ears of the world, your very own home studio. Fear not, I'm here to guide you through that transformative journey from 'what if' to 'what is'.

First things first, consider your space. You don't need a castle; a cozy nook will do just fine. It's not about the size; it's the vibe that counts. Whether it's the corner of your bedroom or an actual spare room, make sure it's a place where you feel at ease, your creative sanctuary. A spot where the rest of the world fades away, and it's just you and the music.

Now, let's talk gear. There's no need to break the bank — start with the essentials. A reliable computer is your musical command center, the heart of operations. It's where you'll arrange, record, and mix, so make sure its specs can handle your software of choice.

Speaking of software, you'll need what's known as a Digital Audio Workstation (DAW). This is the canvas on which you'll paint your sonic landscapes. Plenty of options exist, and many offer free trial periods. Dip your toes in and find the one that feels like home.

Next up, an audio interface — the bridge between the analogue warmth of your voice or instrument and the crisp digital realm. A simple two-channel interface will often suffice for solo acts, whilst bands may need a couple more inputs. Again, you don't need the fanciest kit; clarity and reliability are your watchwords here.

Mics are like spectacles; different lenses for different visions. A solid condenser microphone can capture the nuances of your voice, and if you're feeling more lo-fi or raw, a dynamic mic might just be your ticket. One or two mics, to begin with, will serve you well.

Don't forget those cables! While they might not be glamorous, good quality cabling can save you a world of static and frustration. Then there are headphones — your own personal monitors. Closed-back headphones will keep your recordings free of bleed, letting you hear the truth, and nothing but the truth.

Monitors, the speakers that tell no lies, are vital for understanding how your music truly sounds, outside the confines of earphones and car stereos. You're aiming for transparent, flat response monitors that don't flatter the sound but reveal it in its raw form.

With the key components in place, address the acoustics. Unwanted reverb or echo can toy with your perception of a mix. If you're starting out, some well-placed acoustic foam or even heavy curtains can dampen a lively room, and a rug can do wonders for those harsh floor reflections.

An overlooked hero is the humble music stand or a sturdy desk — a throne for your laptop or a sanctuary for your notepad and pen. Think ergonomics here; the less you strain, the longer you can sustain those creative sessions.

Let's talk ambiance. Set the mood with some lighting that inspires you, maybe a plant here or a piece of art there, anything that makes the space uniquely yours. Your environment should spark inspiration, not snuff it out.

At this juncture, it's worth mentioning power. A surge protector will be one of the best investments for your studio. It shields your precious gear from unexpected power spikes and offers a central hub to manage all your power needs.

While we're protecting things, consider your data. A sturdy external hard drive will safeguard your songs, your digital soul, from the whims of technology. Regular backups are like love letters to your future self.

Once you've got all your gear in place, it's time to test. Record something, anything, and walk it down different listening lanes. See how it fares on a car stereo, earbuds, a home entertainment system. Learn your room's quirks, your gear's character. This will be your laboratory, where you'll invent and perfect your sonic creations.

Finally, remember, the value of your studio is not in the price of your gear but in the comfort it brings to your process. A home studio is an extension of your creative soul, a place where you're free to experiment without judgement. Honour that, cherish it, and above all, make it your own.

So, there you have it. Step by step, you're setting up more than just a studio; you're crafting a realm where ideas take flight, and songs come to life. It's your space in this wide world of sound, a place where you call the shots and the songs come to call. Embrace it, enjoy it, and dance in the limitless possibilities it brings.

Chapter 12:
Protecting Your Work and Copyright

So you've laid down your soul in melodies, you've bared your heart in lyrics, and heck, if your song isn't a snug reflection of your very essence. Now, imagine this snippet of your soul being used somewhere, and not a penny nor a whisper of credit floats back to you. That, my friend, is a songwriter's nightmare come to fluorescent life. Hence, let's skip the nightmare and get straight to the armoury where you'll learn to shield your creative works with the ironclad force of copyright law. It's the spell you cast to keep your musical babies tucked safely in your intellectual arms. Now I know, the mere mention of 'copyright law' can make your eyes glaze over like a doughnut in a baker's window, but stick with me—we're translating legalese to plain old English so you can confidently strut through the rights and wrongs of protecting your artistic progeny. Trust me; once you've got the hang of it, copyright becomes less of a dragon and more of an overgrown lizard in a fancy suit. It's about slaying fears with knowledge, and ensuring that your tunes carry your name, your legacy, and most importantly, your stamp of ownership. After all, what's the point of casting your songs like spells into the wild if you can't claim the magic as your own?

Understanding Copyright Law in the world of songwriting is not just about dotting 'i's and crossing 't's. It's about wrapping your creation in a cloak of protection, where the vibrant tapestry of melody and words you've spun from your soul can't be unraveled by any Tom, Dick, or Harriett with sticky fingers and a tape recorder.

So let's get into the belly of the beast, shall we? When you create an original piece of music, a magical thing happens, quite akin to the universe bestowing upon you a star in the night sky. This star - your song - is your property, something you inherently own from the moment it's fixed in a tangible medium such as a recording or sheet music. That's copyright kicking in, and it's what keeps your star shining in your name alone.

Now, hold on, let's not get muddled with terms. Copyright isn't a flashy badge that declares 'I'm the boss'. It's a legal right granted by law that prevents others from copying or making a meal out of your work without your say-so. You've put your heart and sweat into birthing a tune; wouldn't you want a say in who dances to it?

In most places around our spinning world, like a record on a turntable, copyright lasts for a long time after you've left the stage - typically until 70 years after you've taken your final bow. That's a lot of encores. It means your songs can live on, touching hearts and, yes, potentially filling pockets, long after you've crooned your last note.

But what is a right without knowing how to wield it? Understanding the scope of your copyright is key. It grants you the exclusive right to do a whole host of things: reproduce the song, distribute it, perform it publicly, and even make derivative works. Fancy a remix or a sequel? That's your prerogative.

However, don't get it twisted; copyright doesn't cover everything. It doesn't protect ideas, facts, or that common chord progression you've used that's older than your grandmother's best china. It's the unique way you express your ideas - the melody, the lyrics, the particular arrangement of harmonic delights - that gets the cover.

You might be wondering, 'Do I need to register my song to have copyright protection?' Not necessarily, dear heart. In many countries, copyright exists from the moment of creation. But here's where smart moves pay off. Registering your work grants you a battalion of legal advantages in case of a dispute. Think of it as putting a fortress around your star.

And disputes can arise, like ants at a picnic. Someone may use your song without permission, or perhaps there's a misunderstanding over who wrote what in a collaborative gunfight of creativity. In these instances, the law is your trusty steed, and you better know how to ride it.

Speaking of collaboration, when two or more maestros band together to write a song, it creates a joint copyright. It's like a shared star that you all can wish upon. This means that unless agreed otherwise, any party can exploit the work but - and here's the zinger - the profits should be split. So make sure you're all singing from the same hymn sheet before you start making beautiful music together.

If you're now scratching your head, fretting over how you'd prove your song is your own, fear not. Keep records of your creation process. Date your recordings, scribble on your lyric sheets, email drafts to yourself - create a paper trail as thick as Mississippi mud that shows you were the one turning the wheels in this mill.

But what if you want to share your music with the world, let it fly free like a pigeon from Trafalgar Square? There are avenues for that; enter stage left: copyright licensing. This allows others to use your work in a controlled manner. You can dictate the terms, the where, the how, and the financial nitty-gritty. It's like letting someone borrow your crown, but with a strict note saying 'handle with care' and 'return by midnight'.

Now, if your song lands in the ears of an advertiser who wants to use it to peddle their wares, or a filmmaker desperate to feature it as their leading lady walks away in slow motion, that's when copyright can ring the cash register too. Sync licensing is where your song is synchronized with visual media. Your star fits into their galaxy, but remember, you lay down the orbit.

But let's not get lost in dreams of grandeur. Copyright infringement is a sad tune many musicians have played. If you find your work has been used without permission, seek advice, consult the legal maestros, and remember, the law is your sheet music in this regard.

And remember, time may tick tock, and your star may eventually dim when those 70 posthumous years run out. When copyright expires, your song becomes public domain. It means that your tune joins the chorus of humanity's legacy, free for all to sing, like 'Happy Birthday'. It's a bittersweet symphony, but one that reminds us that music, in the end, belongs to the hearts of the world.

So there you have it, a whistle-stop tour of the wild and wily world of copyright law in songwriting. Keep your wits sharp, and your rights sharper, for the songs you craft today could be the anthems, the lullabies, or the whispered sweet nothings of generations to come.

Registering and Protecting Your Songs Now that you've sent your melodies and lyrics out to play nicely with the world, don't you think it's time to talk about the playground rules? It's a wild, spinning globe of tunes out there, and registering and protecting your songs is the suit of armour they need to navigate it safely.

Imagine this: the seeds of your soul, sown into a beautiful bouquet of sounds and words, catching a breeze and flying into another's hands—a little too boldly, perhaps. Suddenly, someone claims your daisies as their roses. It's not only disheartening but also potentially damaging to your career as a songwriter.

So, let's chat about copyright. In its essence, copyright is like telling the world, "I made this, and you can't have it without my say-so." When you create a piece of music, the moment it's fixed in a tangible medium—like recorded onto your phone or scribbled on a napkin—it's copyrighted. That's right; creativity instantly transforms into a legally recognised form.

But don't rest on your laurels just yet. To truly pack a punch and protect your works, you must register your copyright. It's like rolling up with a megaphone and announcing your claim. In the UK, this means getting in touch with the Intellectual Property Office (IPO). They're the gatekeepers that take your claim and file it neatly into the public record. Once registered, no one can claim ignorance about who the true mastermind is behind your songs.

Filing for copyright registration isn't exactly a walk in the park, but it's nowhere near scaling Mount Everest either. You'll need to provide a copy of your work, fill out some forms, and yes, part with a bit of cash. But think of it as investing in an invisible shield for your music. It's the kind of investment that pays for itself in peace of mind and security.

Now, while you're mulling over the idea of registration, there's also the matter of something called 'performing rights'. If you want your tunes to live their best life and earn their keep while they're at it, registering with a performing rights organisation (PRO) is a must. In the UK, this means entities like PRS for Music. They make sure that when your song plays in a lift, on the radio, or at a sweaty late-night gig, you get the quid you so rightfully deserve.

But let's not forget our dear friends, the co-writers and collaborators. If you're sharing the driver's seat on the song creation expressway, make sure you've got an agreement. Who owns what? How will profits be shared? Hammer out these details upfront. A simple handshake and a nod might feel rockstar now, but it won't hold up if a dispute rears its ugly head.

Let's talk mechanical rights and sync licenses too. If someone wants to record a cover of your song or feature it in a film, these rights come into play. They're called 'mechanical' because back in the day, music was mechanically reproduced (mind-blowing, right?). Sync rights, on the other hand, is all about getting your track in sync with some visual media. It could be a movie, an advert, or even a grumpy cat compilation on YouTube.

And here's a piece of advice as golden as the sun's rays on a summer afternoon: keep everything. Every napkin scribble, every voice note, every email exchange about your songwriting process. It's evidence of your creative journey should anyone challenge your ownership. These little breadcrumbs can lead you back to your rightful throne if things go awry.

Moreover, navigating the nuances of digital rights is like wrestling with the wind—tricky, but not impossible. With streaming giants and digital platforms being the main avenues for music consumption, ensuring you understand how your rights work in the digital realm is key.

But what happens if, despite all your protections, someone covers your song without so much as a by-your-leave, or worse—takes the entire melody and passes it off as their own? Well, don't go starting a fight just yet. You've got the law on your side, and a good solicitor can help you set things right. Legal action should always be a last resort, but it's comforting to know that it's there if you need it.

For the worldly wanderers among songwriters, remember that copyright law varies from country to country. If your music has legs and decides to take a jaunt overseas, familiarise yourself with international copyright treaties and organisations. The Berne Convention, for example, keeps an eye on your intellectual property on foreign soil.

When all's said and sung, registering and protecting your songs isn't just about throwing up barricades around your work. It's about respecting and honouring the very essence of your creativity. It's a declaration that what you create matters and deserves to be safeguarded.

So there you have it, the lowdown on locking down your masterpieces. It's like knitting a warm, cozy jumper for your songs. It might take some effort, but once done, they can go out and conquer the world without catching a cold. Take these steps to heart, wear that jumper with pride, and keep spinning the threads of your musical tapestry.

Remember, the music you create is a fingerprint on the universe—unique, invaluable, and irrefutably yours. Treat it with the care it deserves, and it will sing your name across the heavens and dance floors for eternity.

Chapter 13:
Continuing the Journey in Songwriting

As we come to the close of this lyrical odyssey, it feels rather like setting down one guitar only to pick up another. Songwriting isn't just a chapter in our lives; it's a constant companion, trotting alongside us, rhythmically nudging us to translate the hum of the world into melody and verse. If this book has been the map, then your journey – that endless, rolling road drenched in the golden hues of dawn and dusk – is the one you embark on with every word you scribe and every note you breathe to life.

You've been immersed in the essence of songwriting, found ways to dance with your musical imagination, and you've grasped the building blocks that give our songs backbone and spirit. There's a spark in you, isn't there? A spark that's been fanned into a roaring flame. You've got this. You can weave together harmony and technology, wrap yourself in rhythm, and bedeck your creations with lyrical tales that only you can tell. And remember, every great storyteller once stood precisely where you're standing now: on the brink of something thrillingly unknown.

You now understand that songwriting is as variable as the sea – sometimes you'll ride the waves with the ease of a seasoned sailor, other times you'll fight the torrent to stay afloat. But isn't it the challenge that makes it so invigorating? Keep that rudder steady, balanced by the keystones of structure and form, and you'll harness the currents that seek to unsettle you.

The sonic palette awaits your distinctive touch, and the vast landscape of instruments and arrangements now lies within your grasp. Colour your songs with the shades and tones of your choosing, for you are the artist and your compositions are your masterpieces. Keep in mind that the only true mistake is the fear of striking the wrong chord, for every dissonance can be the birthplace of beautiful innovation.

Through the ebb and flow of the songwriting process, you've learned not just to expect the unexpected, but to embrace it. Like an unexpected chord that somehow fits perfectly, or a lyric that slips out that feels like it was written by the universe itself. Hold on to the knowledge that the trials along the way are simply stepping stones leading you towards mastery.

Commit to collaboration with the knowledge that multiple pens can etch verses no single pen could dream. There's beauty in confluence, a harmonic convergence of minds that can amplify the whisper of an idea into a chorus that resounds across open fields. Two hearts, after all, often beat with more vigour than one.

Turn to your home studio as the sanctuary for your craft, where your songs can be dressed in their Sunday best, ready to dance into the world. Let production be the lens that brings everything into focus, clarifying the view until the panorama before you is as sharp as a high-definition dream.

Shield your creations with the vigor of a guardian, understanding copyright as the armour that safeguards your proverbial children. Let the legalities not daunt you, but rather bolster your confidence, as one who knows their treasures well-protected.

And when you feel as though you're gasping for inspiration, revisit the chapters of this book like old friends. There's wisdom in the wandering and sometimes, retracing your steps can unearth hidden treasures you passed by unwittingly the first time. Sing your melodies, let your metaphors unfurl as you recall how it all started with a single note, a lone word, a solitary beat.

Forge ahead into the world, knowing that the art of songwriting is an ever-evolving conversation between you and your muse, between you and your fellow wanderers, between you and the sprawling canvas that begs for your touch. Resist the lure of complacency by continually seeking out new sounds, novel experiences, and insightful narratives.

Do not mistake the end of this book for the end of your journey. The truth is, the beautiful dance of songwriting is one that has no final bow, no curtain call. Each day is an encore, another chance to write the song that will resonate within the halls of time, long after your hands have ceased to play.

Remember that songwriting is an act of giving - an offering to humanity that can soothe, inspire, provoke, and connect. The world needs your songs, those unspoken sentiments that you dare to voice, the cries of joy and sorrow that you shape into harmony. Your contributions add yet another rich layer to the tapestry of human expression.

So carry on, brave composer of worlds yet to be discovered. Your symphony is endless, your audience boundless. Throw your soul over the strings, and as the echoes of your existence ripple out, know that you are part of something grand – a universal choir where every voice, every verse, every vibration is essential.

You are not merely a songwriter; you are a storyteller, a dream weaver, a keeper of the beat that pulses through the very heart of life. This isn't merely a calling; it's a lifelong voyage, and you, my friend, are destined to sail its melodies with boundless heart and unyielding passion. Lift your voice, let it soar upon the staves, and let the music play on...

Now go forth. The blank sheet awaits. The silence anticipates your next stroke of genius. Continue your journey in songwriting with gusto, grace, and undying love for the craft. May your songs be seeds scattered to the wind, finding fertile ground in the hearts that yearn for them. The journey is never over, it simply sings a new tune. Embrace it. Live it. Write it. And let the music take you where words alone cannot.

Appendix A:
Songwriting Resources and Tools

So you've travelled the melodic paths, waded through harmonic rivers, and climbed the rhythmic mountains. Now, where does one find the right tools to capture the essence of all those adventures? Fret not, in the hidden trove that is Appendix A, you'll discover a treasure chest filled with the gear and gizmos essential for your songcrafting odyssey.

Your Trusty Sidekick: The Notepad

Whether you're old-school with a spiral-bound beauty or swiping through an app like Evernote, never underestimate the might of the humble notepad. It's the keeper of random lyric ideas, the shelter for melodic scribbles, and the incubator where your songs often take their first breaths.

Mighty Melodic Instruments

Piano or Keyboard: The timeless favour - great for fleshing out chords and sparking melodies.

Guitar: Another classic choice - six strings to strum the heart of your song into existence.

Ukulele: For a dose of joy and whimsy, perfect to inject a unique flavour into your tune.

Software That Sings

Stepping into digital terroir, a plethora of software awaits to cater to your every songwriting whim:

DAWs - Digital Audio Workstations like Logic Pro, Ableton Live, or GarageBand are your canvas and brush in one. They let you record, edit, and produce your musical visions.

Songwriting Apps - Sibelius or Noteflight for scoring and MuseScore for composition, because sometimes, you've got to see those notes on the good ol' stave.

Lyric Idea Generators - Apps like Rhymers Block or online rhyming dictionaries, because even the wittiest wordsmiths get stuck on a rhyme sometimes.

Online Realms of Resources

Dive into forums, join songwriting groups or trawl through YouTube tutorials. Exchange ideas on platforms like Reddit's r/Songwriting or the Songwriter's Forum. Oh, and don't miss out on the plethora of MOOCs (Massive Open Online Courses) from platforms like Coursera or Skillshare, where industry pros often share their trade secrets.

Metronomes and Tuners

No matter your instrument, staying in time and in tune is non-negotiable. Good thing there's an app – or a dozen – for that. Cleartune, Tempo, and Metronome Beats are respected shoulders to lean on.

Recording Devices

From the voice memo function on your smartphone to field recorders like the Zoom H1n, make sure you're set to capture inspiration when it strikes, whether you're in a cafe or under the stars.

And there you have it, a baedeker for songwriting mastery. Each songwriter's toolkit will be as unique as their voice, so mix and match these resources to suit your rhythm and flow. The journey of songcraft is ongoing; let these tools be the companions that help you to express, refine, and share your sonic tales with the world.

Glossary of Songwriting Terms

So you've been riding the waves of melody and diving deep into the sea of harmonies. Along the way, you've encountered a symphony of terms that are as colourful and dynamic as the songs themselves. Let's take a moment to put a spotlight on the lexicon of the songwriting world. This glossary, much like a trusty compass, will help steer you through the lingo that shapes the essence of music composition. Let's navigate these waters together, shall we?

A

Arrangement: The art of deciding who plays what, when. It's like a grand conductor guiding the instruments to create a cohesive sonic story.

Arpeggio: A broken chord where the notes are played or sung in sequence, rather than simultaneously. It's the twinkle in the star of a chord's eye.

ASCAP: One of the organizations making sure your pen's might is rewarded right, American Society of Composers, Authors, and Publishers.

B

Backbeat: The steady pulse in your tunes, usually found on the second and fourth beats, giving soul to the rhythm.

Ballad: A song that's usually slow, telling stories of love and heartache, making you feel all the feels.

Bridge: A section of the song that provides contrast, often a musical detour that eventually brings you back home to the chorus or verse.

C

Chord Progression: It's the backbone of your song's harmony, a sequence of chords that sets the emotional runway for your melodies to take flight.

Chorus: That catchy part of the song that seems to echo in your mind's amphitheatre long after the song has ended.

Composition: The very act of creating music, weaving together melody, harmony, and rhythm to tell your story.

D

Dissonance: A tension or clash resulting from the combination of two disharmonious notes. Think of it as the spice in your musical stew.

Dynamics: The louds and softs of your song, shaping the drama and intensity of your musical narrative.

E

Earworm: A song or tune so catchy that it 'crawls' into your brain and 'replays' itself into sweet (or maddening!) oblivion.

F

Fill: A short musical phrase, usually tossed in to garnish the spaces between vocal lines or to lead into a new section of the song.

G

Genre: The category that defines the style of your music. It's like the neighbourhood your song lives in, from rock to reggae, classical to country.

Groove: The irresistible gravitational pull that gets your toes tapping and your head nodding. It's the spirit of the rhythm.

H

Hook: The musical idea that snags the listener's ear and reels them in. Often the most memorable part of a song.

Harmony: The vertical dimension to melody. When notes are stacked together in agreement, they create the harmony — the 'sauce' to your melody's 'pasta'.

I

Improvisation: The art of composing on the fly, often letting the moment dictate the music. Think jazz solos painting with sound.

K

Key: The group of notes that serves as the home base for your song, a cornerstone for building your melodic and harmonic house.

L

Lyrics: The words to your song, crafting tales & emotions that dance with the music. They're the heart speaking to the heart.

M

Melody: The series of notes that sing the main tune, the face of your song that walks into the room first.

Meter: The rhythmic structure of your song, the scaffold that supports the building blocks of your musical edifice.

O

Outro: The swan song of your track, a musical wave goodbye. It's the opposite of an intro; where you tie up all the loose ends and let the curtains fall.

P

Phrasing: How you express the notes and words, giving them shape and feeling. The very breath of your song.

Producer: Like a creative alchemist turning the lead of your musical ideas into the gold of a finished track.

Progression: The sequence of chords marching down the song's pathway, enticing the listener to follow.

R

Rhythm: The heartbeat of the music, what makes your body sway and your pulse race with excitement.

Refain: A line or lines that repeat at certain intervals within your song, giving listeners a familiar home to return to.

S

Stanza: Much like a paragraph in a story, it's a grouped set of lines in your song, usually with a recurring pattern of both rhythm and rhyme.

Syncopation: Upsetting the natural flow of rhythm by accenting the unexpected. It's the surprise party in your song's rhythm.

V

Verse: Sets the stage and tells the story, often guiding the listener verse by verse towards the promise land of the chorus.

Vibrato: The pulsating change of pitch that adds emotion and richness to the singing voice. A butterfly's wings on a note's breeze.

And there you have it, a treasure trove of terms that's yours to explore and master. With these in your songwriting toolkit, you're more than ready to sail the seas of sound and carve your name on the shores of musical history. Just remember, while tools and terms give us the map, it's the spirit and the journey that mold the legends. Onward to adventure!

Appendix B:
Sample Songwriting Agreements and Contracts

So, you've delved into the heart and soul of crafting a song with the patience of a seasoned artist, and now you're looking to share your creations with the world or perhaps with fellow musicians. What's next, you may wonder. Well, picture yourself at the crossroads of creativity and the nitty-gritty of the business world. It's here where the robust framework of agreements and contracts comes into play to protect your hard work and ensure that the sweet symphony of collaboration doesn't end on a sour note.

Now, it's clear that one doesn't wade into the depths of contractual waters without a sturdy vessel. Consider this appendix that very vessel, providing you with examples of the kind of agreements you might encounter or need in your songwriting adventures. In this rhythmical world of ours, legal ties might look like shackles at first glance, but they're really the anchor that keeps your ship steady in turbulent seas.

Within these samples you'll find terms you might need to negotiate with publishing companies, contracts that spell out royalty splits between co-writers, and other arrangements that might have seemed as complex as a jazz improvisation at first sight. Fear not; once you understand the chords and notes of legal agreements, you'll navigate through them as smoothly as a sweet saxophone solo on a summer's evening.

Songwriting Collaboration Agreement

Imagine you're forming a band, not of musicians, but a band of words and melodies with another songwriter. A Songwriting Collaboration Agreement sets the stage for how the music is written and how the profits are split. Think of it as defining who plays what instrument in your creative ensemble.

Work for Hire Agreement

If your songwriting talents have been enlisted by others for a specific project, the Work for Hire Agreement ensures everyone's on the same page. It defines the scope of your work, payment, and clarifies that the hiring party owns the rights to the material. It's like being a sought-after guest musician who comes in, dazzles, gets the applause, and yes, gets paid for the performance.

Publishing Agreement

Once you have a song ready to touch the hearts and minds of the public, a Publisher might step in like a maestro, promising to take your song to audiences far and wide. The Publishing Agreement outlines who controls the rights, how royalties are split, and the tune to which both you and the publisher dance together in the financial side of the music biz.

Now come on, let's be honest; there's a certain thrill in the thought of your creations sparking life across the airwaves, isn't there? But without these frameworks, your masterpieces might flutter away like notes carried off by the wind. So, take these sample agreements, tailor them to your own symphony of circumstances, and protect your songs as fiercely as a grand piano guards its keys.

Remember, these examples are not to be taken as direct legal advice. They are more like sheet music – a guide, to begin with. Let it be known that the art of songwriting isn't just about the chorus and verses; it's about making sure that when the applause fades and the curtains close, your legacy and livelihood continue to flourish. It's in the echo of a well-negotiated contract that the true longevity of your song can be heard.

So, go ahead, take these sample agreements, and make them your own. Let them be the unsung heroes of your songwriting story, the silent guardians of your works. Let them sing in the key of legal harmony, ensuring your musical journey remains both brilliant and boundless.

Chapter 14:
Acknowledgements

And so, my grand ensemble of words, chords, and insights nears its final note. But before the curtains close on our little symphony of songwriting wisdom, it's essential to doff my hat to the maestros who've orchestrated the possibility of this book seeing the light of day.

First, a standing ovation for my family, whose unwavering belief in me could outshine the sun itself. The late-night musings and early-morning scribblings would've led to naught without the steadfast support of those who share my last name—and quite frequently, my refrigerator.

To the friends who've been my sounding board, thank you for lending your ears and your honest critiques. Your ability to tell me when my melodies meandered off-key or when my lyrics lapsed into cliché has been invaluable.

Let's not forget my fellow songbirds and tune-smiths. To the collaborators who've shared stages and studio booths with me; our joint efforts have always been greater than the sum of our individual talents. In particular, a special mention is necessary for those who turned coffee-fueled jam sessions into three-minute masterpieces.

I tip my hat to the wordsmiths and poets from whom I borrowed inspiration. Your lyrical landscapes and rhythmic roads paved the way for this humble author to tread a musical adventure. Not to usurp your thunder, but to sing in harmony with the echoes of your imagination.

What's next, you might wonder? In the grand tapestry of sounds and silences, I am but a note. There's an entire symphony out there waiting to be written, songs yet to be sung, and stories yet to be told. My commitment is to continue weaving my part, in tune with the inexhaustible muse that music is.

My hope? That in sharing my experiences, others will find the courage to trace their own melodies, navigate their own harmonies, and script their own stories into the annals of song. This book is an invitation, a hand extended to those who dream of crafting songs that might, one day, resonate across the airwaves or within the quiet confines of a listener's heart.

To those who've read this far, who've invested time and heart into the pages of this book: your journey is uniquely your own. Like a fingerprint on a fretboard, each one tells a story. Your story is as valuable and as vital to the great rhyming scheme of life as any other. May your verses be many, and your muse be ever-present.

In closing, remember that the song within you insists on being heard. It beats in your chest, thrums in your veins, and whispers through every breath. Your next song could be the one that speaks for a generation or speaks to a single soul. The beauty lies in the not-knowing, in the potential of every blank page and every pluck of a string.

So here's to the music makers, the dreamers of dreams, the scribblers of hidden tunes. May your songwriting journey be as rich with chords as it is with challenges, for it's in the overcoming that we often compose our greatest works.

Until the next melodic encounter, keep your music genuine, your themes universal, and your storytelling perpetual. The world is waiting for your next song...

A salute is due to the teachers and mentors who sharpened my quill and tuned my intellectual instrument.

The music aficionados who populate the dimly lit corners of vinyl stores and the spirited debates of online forums deserve their bouquets as well. Your passion is the lifeblood of the art we love. Isn't it mellifluous, the way a simple tune can connect stranger souls?

Gratitude must be extended to the technology wizards; the creators of software and hardware that make music production accessible to the masses. Your tools are the anvil upon which I hammer out my musical visions, and your constant innovation keeps the flame of creativity alight.

To the readers who've followed my melodic musings—from the hallowed pages of dog-eared notebooks to the polished paragraphs herein—your engagement fuels my fervor. You are the rhythm section to my lyrical lead; without you, the dance floor would surely be empty.

A head bow to my editor, the steadfast compatriot in combating the dreaded typos and ensuring cohesion, you've sculpted my chaotic thoughts into a narrative that, I hope, sings rather than stutters.

To the unsung heroes of logistics—agents, publishers, and the army of detail-oriented folks who ensure that books don't merely end as thoughts veiled in obscurity—you are the unsung chord progressions that give a song its satisfying resolution.

Let's not let the bar staff, doorkeepers, and stage technicians go unnoticed. Your roles in the theatres of our gigs provide the essential backdrop against which our music revels. Your toils behind the scenes are as critical as the spotlight itself.

Hands together for the tireless legal team, those knights in shining armour who navigate the labyrinthine sprawl of copyright law so that creatives may sleep soundly. Your work ensures melodies and words remain rightfully tethered to their creators' names.

And in a gentle decrescendo, a nod to the quiet muses of nature— stormy skies, rolling hills, and whispering streams. You've lent me metaphors and motifs aplenty. Just as music is woven into every aspect of life, so life weaves its narratives into my music.

Lastly, an echo of thanks to you, dear songspinner, who dares to dream in staves and clefs. May the chorus of advice in these pages accompany you on your odyssey. Here's to your future harmonies and the stories they will unfurl. In the great symphony of life, may your song ever soar.

Chapter 15:
About the Author

Picture this: a young kid, tapping out rhythms on the kitchen table, humming melodies while the kettle sings in harmony. That's where this journey begins. From the cluttered backstreets of a bustling metropolis came a passion for the intangible magic spun from chords and lyrics. It began not with a bang, but a tune. As that kid, I scrawled lyric upon napkin, notebook, and even the back of my hand. Little by little, a songwriter was born.

The path from there was rich with melody and oftentimes discordant. I'd spend countless evenings with my face half-lit by the glow of a computer screen, diving into forums where other music enthusiasts bemoaned their creative blocks or celebrated their latest composition. Those forums felt like salons of the past, where artists and thinkers would gather to sharpen each other's minds and talents.

In between the chords learned and the lyrics penned, life unfolded its own set of lessons. There were adventures and misadventures, love found in chords, and heartbreak in minor keys. These experiences became the bedrock of my storytelling, and each song was a chapter of an ever-evolving narrative. I delved deep into the craft, not just to create but to understand the why and the how of every note and every word.

Over time, I traded the kitchen table for modest stages, where the microphone felt like both a beacon and an interrogator under the spotlight. There's nothing quite like the first time you share your songs with an audience, feeling every shifting presence, every cough, every cheer. These were moments of affirmation and moments that brought doubts; they were raw, real, and utterly unforgettable.

Then came the collaborations. Let me tell you, there's a thrill that comes from merging minds with other creators. Each partnership was like discovering a new dialect in the language of music. Weaving my story into someone else's story, we'd create tapestries richer than what either of us could craft alone. I learned that songwriting, at its heart, is also about listening—really listening—to the perspectives that life and its myriad players have to offer.

Not every day was part of a meteoric rise. In fact, many were spent troubleshooting tech in a home studio that resembled a tangle of cables and ambitions. Yet, even those days were underscored by a beat, a rhythm that drove me to push through the frustrations of a mix that just wouldn't sit right or a melody that refused to stick.

With time, I became something of a custodian of my own creations, navigating the tricky waters of copyright law to keep my songs safe in a world that's as rife with piracy as it is with opportunity. Protecting one's work is like nurturing a child. It's intensive, it's necessary, and it's all worth it when you see your creations stride out into the world.

And here's something vital: the songwriting path has also been one of constant learning. Be it through scratching errors and correcting courses, or embracing the fluidity of a craft that refuses to stagnate. Trends come and go, technology evolves, but the essence of creating something from nothing remains an immutable triumph.

My story is not singular. It's echoed in the experiences of countless others who've felt the inexorable pull of music. These pages you've just journeyed through aren't just from my mind; they're an amalgam of the collective wisdom of every mentor, peer, and yes, even critic I've encountered. In truth, we're all students of the music we adore and servants to the songs we birth.